# FIRE
# RAIN

# FIRE RAIN

*Breaking Spiritual Containments*
*With Precision Prayers*

ALEXANDER O. EMOGHENE

# CONTENTS



## SECTION 1: WHAT IS PRAYER



## SECTION 2: WHY DO WE PRAY?

## SECTION 3: BEWARE OF EVIL INTERACTIONS



## SECTION 4: PRECISION PRAYERS

# PREFACE

he world is moving into its fifth industrial revolution as we know it. Every revolution introduced humanity into a new culture and a way of living.

Usually, a few individuals respond positively to enable the transitions. They are call shapers and doers. Often time these individuals are bold to challenge the status-quo. Though possessing several flaws and limitation, they are willing to challenge those boundaries, barriers and limitation which resists their leadership qualities to become leaders in their chosen field

This fifth industrial revolution generation will be led by people who think and leads other to discover purpose above profit. This will be in the impact generation. A generation seeking the good of the world, and seeking how to share the earth effectively to serve humanity.

They will answer the purpose question for the world. They will help bring meaning to all prior industrial revolution combined.

Containers, serve the purpose to preserve the integrity of content, for safe delivery to end users. However, the content will remain useless if the container remains sealed. See your gift and talent as a precious content, wrapped in the containers of time, comfort, ignorance, disappointment, pain, low-self-esteem and in human skin but the world is waiting eagerly to receive and enjoy your content.

Breaking containments, is a requirement; is a necessity; if you want to become significant in life to serve the world with what God has loaded you with.

You were born for a reason and must challenge all containing factors, so the world can enjoy the gift of God in you.

This book attempts to profile spiritual forces the enemy sanctions in operation around individuals and on paths of life to contain and prevent growth, development, excellence, leadership and productivity; from truly maximizing your God given potential.

These prayers were birth out of a 15 day, fasting and prayers marathon in our ministry. During which the Lord instructed to put into print. As you go through and as He leads you in prayer; I pray all containing spirits and their stronghold will be broken for good as you embrace your significance in Jesus Name.

# DEDICATE

I dedicate this book to the Holy Spirit. To your
patience, instruction and inspiration.

I could not have gone through this period of my life with you.

I praise You Fathers, For Your Love and Tender Mercies

Jesus I Love you.

Thank you

# ACKNOWLEDGMENTS

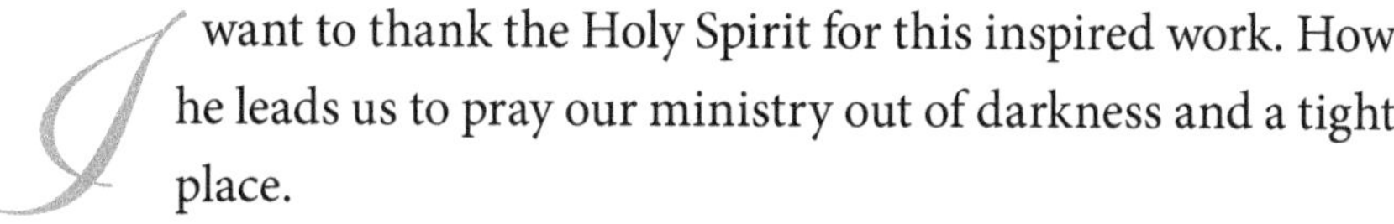

I want to thank the Holy Spirit for this inspired work. How he leads us to pray our ministry out of darkness and a tight place.

I want to appreciate my precious wife Judith for her love, enthusiasm and prayers. Thank you, for the time and space you allow me to have during the preparatory season. You give me the courage to keep on writing.

# FIRE-RAIN

The purpose of this prayer-rain book is to lead you to possess the know-how of displacing demonic entities and demonic activities from a family, business, church, city or an area. In the course of going through this book, you will encounter words liker die, destroying demonic road blocks, demonic influence, and pulling down strong-holds. Understand, therefore, that whilst you are praying these prayers, satan will try to lie to you that demon spirits do not die or cannot die –

(Luke 4:34) says, Let us alone; what have we to do with thee, thou Jesus of Nazareth? art thou come to **destroy** us? I know thee who thou art; the Holy One of God.

DESTROY... (apollumi) to destroy fully (reflexively, to perish, or lose), literally or figuratively:--destroy, die, lose, mar, perish.

(Ps 91:13) Thou shalt tread upon the lion and adder: the young lion and the dragon shalt thou trample under feet.

Isaiah 63 is a messianic scripture that deals with how the Messiah will trample over his enemies and destroy them; and we see how He will show up covered with blood, having all of His enemies totally destroyed.

Technically, spirits do not die, BUT when we say "died" it means they stop or cease to exist in all areas concerning you and your affairs. It means:

- We refuse them the ability to exist and influence our life
- We refuse their presence to reign over us
- We refuse them the audience to participate in the affairs concerning us as believers
- We destroy their activities in and around our domain
- We refuse them the right to exit to be able to execute their ungodly activities

With this understanding, pray the following prayers with total conviction and authority. Authoritatively declare your victory without worries whether satan and his cohorts can or cannot be destroyed… because they can surely be destroyed - even in your situation. Your prayer rains down that power into effect… your prayer causes that fire-rain to begin to come down… your prayer releases that fire-rain to burn down all forces against your God-given destiny.

The following are powerful prayers specifically designed to bring true deliverance and freedom to the praying person… deliverance from the strong hold of satan.

# WHAT IS PRAYER

# PRAYER IS A TWO-WAY COMMUNICATION WITH GOD

Communication is the means of sending or receiving information. By definition, communication is a dialogue not a monologue. It is a mean where information is exchanged between two or more parties. In prayer, we get to communicate to God. (Luke 11:2). Often time people forget that God is a person desiring relationship and He desires to interact with us in every way possible.

God made Adam in other to have a relationship with him. By providing a safe and healthy environment for Adam, God will walk in the cool of the day to have fellowship with Adam. It is by communication that God provided all Adam will ever need. We must realize how important meeting our needs is to Him.

*Jeremiah 33:3...Ask me, and I will tell you things that you don't know and can't find out CEV.*

How about opening up a conversation with God today? By seeing and treating Him as a person. Instead of an empty talk and a religious activity to God without truly hearing Him. Do not be satisfied with just a monologue, and walking away, feeling that He has heard you and that is it. There is more, when you pray. Prayer is a heart to heart time with a loving father. A time to interact, to follow, to be corrected and to be directed. It is an engagement time highly prioritize by God.

> *Matthew 6:6-8...When you pray, go into a room alone and close the door. Pray to your Father in private. He knows what is done in private and will reward you. When you pray, don't talk on and on as people do who don't know God. They think God likes to hear long prayers. Don't be like them. Your Father knows what you need even before you ask*

# Chapter 2

# PRAYER IS A PLACE OF EXCHANGE

Exchange, the act of giving something to someone and them giving you something else. God invites us to exchange our troubles, fears and lack for His solutions. In prayer, we get to hear and see the possibilities of exchange and we go for it.

In Isaiah, we are shown the possibility of exchange;

> *Isaiah 61:3...To appoint unto them that mourn in Zion, to give unto them beauty for ashes, the oil of joy for mourning, the garment of praise for the spirit of heaviness, that they might be called trees of righteousness, the planting of the* LORD, *that He might be glorified."*

In prayer, we get to exchange our needs for His answers, and we also begin to understand that most things that we need are not just going to show up by default. Needs are met by going to the place where such needs are made available. For example, if you have some money and needs groceries, you will have to go to the grocery store for an exchange. To pray is as showing up in the place of abundance. I will like to point out that faith in God is your medium of exchange. This is the essence of these below prayer book points; they are to help, lift you up and to add value to your faith.

*(Hebrew 4:16) Let us therefore come boldly unto the throne of grace, that we may obtain mercy, and find grace to help in time of need.*

# PRAYER POINT

- ➤ Remove all obstacles to this great exchange
- ➤ Remove all fear of rejection
- ➤ Remove all timidity of the soul and spirit
- ➤ Remove all preconceived notions of how God will answer you.
- ➤ Receive and open the lines for better communication
- ➤ Re-establish your confidence in the Grace of God
- ➤ Re-establish your confidence in the mercies of God
- ➤ Re-establish your confidence in the provision of God

# Chapter 3

# PRAYER IS A SPIRITUAL ACTIVITY

Activity is the condition in which things are happening or being done. This reminds me of working out in the gym, it's a sound of activity. Everyone is active on the different parts of their body structure according to the work out plan for the day.

Something is happening as we pray; it is an activity in the spiritual realms. It is not a mental exercise; it is a spiritual undertaking. You are not just making vocal sounds but as you verbalize and express yourself in the place of prayer, there are spiritual activity going on based on your specific prayer needs.

Other synonyms are pursuit, occupation, venture, undertaking, enterprise, and project. If we can begin to see prayer from such an intention and elevated platform, one that demands consistency and growth, then our whole paradigm will shift into a desire that is more proactive rather that a passive pursuit.

It is a rewarding activity — one with both spiritual and natural benefits. As a spiritual activity, it stands to be the only means by which you can build your spiritual muscles as it were.

*But ye, beloved, building up yourselves on your most*
*holy faith, praying in the Holy Ghost, Jude 1:20.*

These are the words of King David. He is the most successful world leader and the greatest king Israel ever had. His success can be attributed to his spiritual exploits by his desire to be in God's temple to seek the face of God in prayer.

Psalms 27:4...One thing have I desired of the Lord, that will I seek after; that I may dwell in the house of the Lord all the days of my life, to behold the beauty of the Lord, and to enquire in his temple.

# Chapter 4

# PRAYER IS EXCERCING YOUR SPIRITUAL AUTHORITY

I like the definition which google gave to the word Authority. It states, "the power to give orders or make decisions: the power or right to direct or control someone or something. The confident quality of someone who knows a lot about something or who is respected or obeyed by other people.

Genesis 1:26. And God said, Let us make man in our image, after our likeness: and let them have dominion over the fish of the sea, and over the fowl of the air, and over the cattle, and over all the earth, and over every creeping thing that creepeth upon the earth.

From the above scripture verse, we gain the wisdom that God's original plan for humanity was not only to have natural mastery of the earth but spiritual mastery as well. Humanity was locked in Adam when God commission man to have dominion over all the earth.

In prayer, we exercise these spiritual powers and privileges to give and make a decision concerning the things we need to accomplish for God on the earth. Prayer is the key to openly establish control over the enemy's plans and strategy.

*Luke 10:19..."Behold, I have given you authority to tread on serpents and scorpions, and over all the power of the enemy, and nothing will injure you. NASB*

Prayer also is where we use our absolute power to get results. The text below talks about how tremendous power is released in the place of prayer. There is a strong commission on dominion when it comes to ruling and reigning with God. His intention is for you to step up to the place of authority over evil forces and bring the kingdom of God on earth.

*(James 5:16) Confess to one another therefore your faults (your slips, your false steps, your offense, your sins) and PRAY [also] for one another that you may be healed and restored [to a spiritual tone of mind and heart]. The earnest ((heartfelt, continued) prayer of a righteous man makes tremendous power available [dynamic in its working] AMP*

# PRAYER POINT

- ➤ I step into my office of absolute power right NOW!
- ➤ I step into my right to petition heaven
- ➤ I step into my secret place with my heavenly Father
- ➤ I step into use my power of attorney to use the name of Jesus
- ➤ I step into the realm of my high calling
- ➤ I step up to pronounce judgment on the enemy
- ➤ I step up to use my power to reign in Christ
- ➤ I step to announce my position in Christ
- ➤ I step up to use the MASTERS KEY today of absolute authority!

*(Mt 16:19) And I will give unto thee the keys of the kingdom of heaven: and whatsoever thou shalt bind on earth shall be bound in heaven: and whatsoever thou shalt loose on earth shall be loosed in heaven.*

# Chapter 5

# PRAYER IS ESTABLISHING YOUR MARK ON THE MAP ON THE EARTH

rayer is establishing a business or a company that will last for a long time. It is also having a permanent base. Do you want to leave a legacy? Do you want to see what your establishments, leave a mark that cannot be erased? Do you want to change live for the Kingdom? Then Prayer gives you the access.

God called you into His kingdom to establish the work of your hands. He called you to become successful and bring permanence to such success.

*(John 15:16) Ye have not chosen me, but I have chosen you, and ordained you, that ye should go and bring forth fruit, and that your fruit should remain: that whatsoever ye shall ask of the Father in my name, he may give it you.*

"that your fruit should remain". God wants His people to experience supernatural stability in a world that seems that nothing is certain. Yet in His kingdom His view of you is that your fruit remains. In everything you accomplish, be it soul winning, kingdom business, relationship, family and church, God desires to establish you.

*Daniel 12: 3...And they that be wise shall shine as the brightness of the firmament; and they that turn many to righteousness as the stars for ever and ever.*

*Matthew 7:24 Therefore whosoever heareth these sayings of mine, and doeth them, I will liken him unto a wise man, which built his house upon a rock: 25 And the rain descended, and the floods came, and the winds blew, and beat upon that house; and it fell not: for it was founded upon a rock. 26 And every one that heareth these sayings of mine, and doeth them not, shall be likened unto a foolish man, which built his house upon the sand: 27 And the rain descended, and the floods came, and the winds blew, and beat upon that house; and it fell: and great was the fall of it.*

# Chapter 6

# PRAYER IS HOW WE MOVE THINGS AROUND IN THE SPIRIT IN ORDER TO AFFECT PHYSICAL THINGS

"The Law of motion states, all things remain at rest until a force is applied. It is a given that things can only move when a certain force is applied. This same principle applies to spiritual things. The devil and his cohorts are unseen demonic forces and they use demonic spiritual materials, strategies and equipment in their effort to stop and contain individuals in all aspects of life.

> *Ephesians 6: 12 For we wrestle not against flesh and blood, but against principalities, against powers, against the rulers of the darkness of this world, against spiritual wickedness in high places.*

So, your prayer is a forceful element to move spiritual things in or out of place as the case may be. When you pray, you avail God an opportunity to move for you. By commissioning angelic ministration to move out evil forces, creating waves of power that destroy spiritual containers. The scripture points to

Acts 4:31...And when they have prayed, the place was shaken where they were assembled together; and they were all filled with the Holy Ghost, and they spake the word of God with boldness

> *"the place was shaken." The high priest and the authority were trying to contain and restrict the spread of the Gospel but thank God for prayers. A few moments before their prayers, the Apostles were warned not to preach openly about Jesus. They were reprimanded, flogged and threatened. An oppressive spirit was released on them, which needed to be moved up and away from the group. After the prayers, the oppressive spirit was moved out and replaced by the spirit of Boldness.*

# PRAYER POINTS

- By Faith I forcefully command all traffic of evil to stop and redirected to hell.
- By Faith I forcefully command all move of evil report to seize and redirected to hell.
- By Faith I forcefully command and move out the mountain of failure and disappointments to hell
- By Faith I forcefully command and move out the mountain of shame and disgrace to hell.
- By Faith I forcefully command and move out the mountain of poverty and lack of sicknesses to hell.

# Chapter 7

# PRAYER IS A SPIRITUAL ACTIVITY WITH NATURAL CONSEQUENCES

Consequence is a result, an outcome or an off-shot. Usually an effect that is really unpleasant and unwanted but it is there. When we engage in active prayer, with the understanding that prayer is an active spiritual activity that is profitable, giving time and place for it, satan begins to receive the consequence of his action on our affairs.

When you pray in the spirit, natural things change. We release the power of God judgment against forces as disease, depression, anxiety, fear and every pain caused by both nature and the enemy

> *1KING 18:42-44...* *[42] So Ahab went up to eat and to drink. And Elijah went up to the top of Carmel; and he cast himself down upon the earth, and put his face between his knees,[43] And said to his servant, Go up now, look toward the sea. And he went up, and looked, and said, There is nothing. And he said, Go again seven*

*times.*[44] *And it came to pass at the seventh time, that he said, Behold, there ariseth a little cloud out of the sea, like a man's hand. And he said, Go up, say unto Ahab, Prepare thy chariot, and get thee down that the rain stop thee not.*

When we pray in the spirit, history is affected. In the place of prayer, we can rewrite what was not in line with the word of God. The Natural realm is connected to the spiritual and the spiritual also governed by it. Therefore, changes or certain movements in the spiritual realm influences a noticeable effect on the natural. The scripture declares, the whole universe is held in place by the word of God. (Hebrew 1: 3). What a privilege to understand, God has given to put such privilege at the disposal of the believer. With such power of prayer, the believer can begin to bring God counsel into history.

- By prayer, Moses changed the course of history. One man connected with God in the place of prayer and he led over 3 million slaves out of captivity and made them a nation of free men. He was known by his people as one who will spend long periods of time in the mountain, communicating with God. The scripture confirms this, when God spoke of Moses, having spoken to him face to face (Exodus 33:11 / Number 12:8

- By prayer, Joshua changed the course of history. In the battle with fives Kings over the valley of Adjalon, nature responded to the prayers of Joshua, as he led his army into victory over 5 kings which came up against their ally, the Gibeonites. Joshua 10:12... On the day the LORD gave the Amorites over to Israel, Joshua said to the LORD in the presence of Israel. "Sun, stand still over Gibeon, and you, moon, over the Valley of Aijalon."

13 So the sun stood still, and the moon stopped, till the nation avenged itself on its enemies, as it is written in the Book of Jashar. The sun stopped in the middle of the sky and delayed going down about a full day.

- By prayer, Elijah changed the course of history. During the course of three years and six months no rainfall was recorded in Israel because Elijah had prayed. He was moved in the realms of spirit to stand against the reign of King Ahab and his wife Jezebel. The couple have allowed unrighteousness through idolatry to gradually sip into all fabrics of the life of God's holy people. James 5:17...Elijah was a human being as we are, and he prayed earnestly that it would not rain, and for three years and six months it did not rain on the land. 18... But when he did pray for rain, it fell from the skies and made the crops grow. CEV.

- By prayer, Elisha changed the course of history. This was when Elisha caused axe to flood on water — defying the very nature of floatation. In the natural, metal that is not constructed to float will sink right to the bottom and remain there. However, Elisha by prayer made an axe head laying at the bottom of a river to float back to the surface.

- By prayer, Jesus changed the course of history. Jesus is the center piece of history. The short time He spent on the earth was so impactful to the point where our calendar is pinned on His time on earth.

# Chapter 8

# PRAYER IS CREATING AN ALTER FOR GOD ON EARTHLY PLACES

lters are sacred places where spirits and humans meet. It is the place where divine and mortals interact to establish law and order. Alters are places of supernatural covenants sealed by blood – breakable only by blood.

*(Genesis 12:7) ...And the LORD appeared unto Abram, and said, Unto thy seed will I give this land: and there* **___builded he an altar unto the LORD___**, *who appeared unto him.*

Any place where consistent prayers are held, becomes a sacred place or alighting premises for the Spirt of God. It never ceases to amaze me, how simple church can slowly because a meeting place for dialogue between divinity and humanity. It is true that any place can become an altar, so long as it is a place of prevailing prayers. Not to talk about a house dedicated to the service of God. That is why church buildings are important and key for local to national revival.

There are different levels of alter:

1. Personal level alters
2. Group level alter
3. Local levelers alter
4. Regional alter
5. National alters
6. Global alter

Altars are mentioned often in the Bible and they can represent many different things. They are places of encounters, forgiveness, prayer, worship, covenant, and remembrance. Where there is an altar, God can alter anyone's story. Alter is also a place of transformation. It was on the mountain where He God took His apostles to pray and His raiment was transfigured.

> *Luke 9:28...And it came to pass about an eight days after these sayings, he took Peter and John and James, and went up into a mountain to pray. [29] And as he prayed, the fashion of his countenance was altered, and his raiment was white and glistering.*

Noah built an altar with his family after the flood and made a sacrifice. Then, God made a covenant with him and his descendants. (Genesis 8-9)

Abram built an altar after God gave him a covenant promise that He would give the land of Israel to Abram's descendants. (Genesis 13)

Isaac built an altar after he re-dug his father's wells and God confirmed His covenant blessing to Isaac because of His pledge to his father, Abraham. (Genesis 26)

Jacob built an altar after God changed his name to Israel and made peace with his brother, Esau. (Genesis 31-33)

Joshua built an altar out of memorial stones when the Children of Israel crossed the River Jordan carrying the Ark. (Joshua 4)

Moses built an altar after he wrote the Torah and God made a covenant with the Children of Israel. (Exodus 24)

These are just a few examples of people building altars throughout antiquity representing the occasion and place where they had a personal encounter with God.

# WHY DO WE PRAY?

# Chapter 9

# WE PRAY BECAUSE WE LIVE IN A SPIRITUAL WORLD

hether saved or unsaved, we all live in a spiritual world, and this calls for spiritual interactions and conflicts. (Ephesians 2:2-3) **...key words - 1. according 2. Conversation'.** There are people who are in a battle but have no clue that they are in one: These people become spiritual casualties. They think that if they put spiritual warfare out of their minds, they will be free from it. In their reasoning, if they remain uninvolved, they will be excused. To them, positive thinking will make everything fine. I am so glad that we know the truth.

Ephesian 6:12...For we wrestle not against flesh and blood, but against principalities, against powers, against the rulers of the darkness of this world, against spiritual wickedness in high places.

The scripture further enlightened us saying, in 1 John 5:19...And we know that we are of God, and **the whole world lieth** in wickedness. This means, so long as you live in this world some wickedness lies close to your door step and its aim is to inflict spiritual injuries which can end up being fatal.

The truth is that we are not just body and soul (mind), but we are also spirit being. Positive thinking alone will not stand up against the enemy's devices. So we need to be spirit-wise and make no provisions for the flesh. (Rom 13:14): But put ye on the Lord Jesus Christ, and **make not provision for the flesh**, to fulfill the lusts thereof.

a. **GOD IS SPIRIT.** John 4:25... God is a Spirit: and they that worship him must worship him in spirit and in truth. 1 Corinthians 14:2... For he that speaketh in an unknown tongue speaketh not unto men, but unto God: for no man understandeth him; howbeit in the spirit he speaketh mysteries.

b. **THE HOLY SPIRIT IS SPIRIT.** John 16:13 Howbeit when he, the Spirit of truth, is come, he will guide you into all truth: for he shall not speak of himself; but whatsoever he shall hear, that shall he speak: and he will shew you things to come.

c. **JESUS IS KNOW BY THE SPIRIT.** Corinthians 5:16.... Wherefore henceforth know we no man after the flesh: yea, though we have known Christ after the flesh, yet now henceforth know we him no more. Act 9:5...And he said, Who art thou, Lord? And the Lord said, I am Jesus whom thou persecutest: it is hard for thee to kick against the pricks.

d. **ANGELS ARE SPIRIT.** Psalms 104:4...Who maketh his angels spirits; his ministers a flaming fire: Hebrews 1:14... Are they not all ministering spirits, sent forth to minister for them who shall be heirs of salvation?

e. **SATAN IS A SPIRIT.** John 13:27...And after the sop Satan entered into him. Then said Jesus unto him, that thou doest, do quickly. Satan being an angel is also a spirit

f. **THE BLESSINGS IS SPIRITUAL** (Ephesian 1:3): Therefore, engaging the force of faith in prayer we make available tremendous power by which we can move spiritual things around and at will. (Read Matthew 21:21/ Mark 11:23)

**g.** **THE CHURCH IS SPIRITUAL** 1 Peter 2:5...Ye also, as lively stones, are built up a spiritual house, an holy priesthood, to offer up spiritual sacrifices, acceptable to God by Jesus Christ.

**h.** **THE WORD IS SPIRIT.** John 6:63...It is the spirit that quickeneth; the flesh profiteth nothing: the words that I speak unto you, they are spirit, and they are life. Ezekiel 2:2... And the spirit entered into me when he spake unto me, and set me upon my feet, that I heard him that spake unto me

**i.** **WORSHIP IN SONGS, DANCE AND INSTRUMENT IS SERVICE IS SPIRITUAL...** Ephesian 5:19...Speaking to yourselves in psalms and hymns and spiritual songs, singing and making melody in your heart to the Lord. Psalms 33... Sing unto him a new song; play skillfully with a loud noise. Psalm 149:3...Let them praise his name in the dance: let them sing praises unto him with the timbrel and harp. Exodus 40:9...And thou shalt take the anointing oil, and anoint the tabernacle, and all that is therein, and shalt hallow it, and all the vessels thereof: and it shall be holy.

**j.** **MAN IS MADE TO BE THE SPIRIT OVERSEE OF THE PLANET.** Genesis 1:26...And God said, Let us make man in our image, after our likeness: and let them have dominion over the fish of the .sea, and over the fowl of the air, and over the cattle, and over all the earth, and over every creeping thing that creepeth upon the earth.

Mankind is built not only to engage in this super spiritual environment but he is to govern and rule over it. It is by prayer and engaging in the revelation of the spiritual realm that we can fully accomplish our assignment.

# Chapter 10

# WE PRAY TO ENTER THE REALMS OF POWER WITH GOD

In prayer, you answer the call of God to rule and reign with Him in authority. When we pray, we access divine power…

*1 Peter 5:11…For all power belongs to God, now and forever. Amen. KJV*

*Psalms 62:11…The True God spoke this once, and twice I've heard: That You, the True God, hold all power; TVoice*

So, as we pray, we uncover and disarm the powers of darkness. By prayer, we stop his plans to further create darkness in the earthly realms by the release of the forces of light. The language of force is the only language satan understands. He is adamant and persistent, therefore, pray to exude powerful force to repel him. Jesus confirms the powers of the enemy in this statement

*Luke 10:19...Look, I have given you the authority to trample on snakes and scorpions and over all the power of the enemy; nothing at all will harm you. CSB*

In prayer, we have access to the amour of God; unlike the amour of Saul which was too heavy for David to wear for the battle with Goliath; God's amour is a perfect fit for the believer who dares to enter into the realms of prayer. This is the amour of light and truth. The revelation of who God is and the plan HE has for the world. Do you feel like putting this powerful amour on? Then step up into the realms of prayer.

(Ephesians 6:11): Put on the whole armour of God, that ye may be able to stand against the **wiles of the devil. (WILES MEANS schemes sought out" for deceiving/ to deceive and destroy...) Romans 13:12...**The night is far spent, the day is at hand: let us therefore cast off the works of darkness, and let us put on the armour of light.

Although satan is availed of certain powers, the believers can stand in the power of God to engage it. This power that the believer has been endowed with is from God to render powerless all the forces hell can put together. It is in your prayer that His divine authority is released. It is in prayer, you walk in the victory of God.

# Chapter 11

# WHEN WE PRAY, WE ARE EMPOWERED TO DESTROY WORKS OF DARKNESS

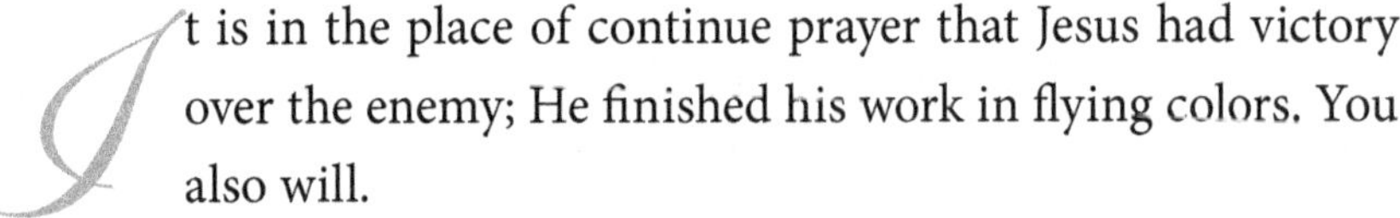

t is in the place of continue prayer that Jesus had victory over the enemy; He finished his work in flying colors. You also will.

The Cambridge dictionary defines to destroy as; to damage something so badly that it cannot be used. The word of God introduces us to the fact that Jesus came to destroy the works of satan. The major work or strategy is to keep the believer contained and limited. Unable to fully express all the glory of God and to break out in all the glory which resides with believing in Christ. Will you allow him to keep you contained and limited?

> *1 John 3:8...He that committeth sin is of the devil; for the devil sinneth from the beginning. For this purpose the Son of God was manifested, that he might destroy the works of the devil. KVJ*

The scripture shows myriads of cases where satan slips in to lie, deceive or mislead individuals to go against the plans of God. For example, Adam and Eve where remove completely of course by one mistake. David caused the death of seventy thousand men because satan stood against Israel and provoked David to number Israel (1 Chronicles 21: 1, 14). We also experience Judas who satan filled up to betray our Lord and savior Jesus Christ. These were satan's attempt to throw in a stick in the wheel, to derail God's plan for these men. Thank God he failed in all his attempt and my prayer is that he will also fail in your life.

When we refuse to pray, we will walk under the impression that all is well and good, but praying exposes these works of satan. The works of darkness simply imply that you will not normally see his plot in the natural eyes, neither will you be able to sense him cognitively. Therefore, you need revelation knowledge to flood your spirit in prayer, to empower your decision and actions.

The mistake we make in life can be avoided, if only we are enlightened and know the right steps to follow in the midst of myriads of option. Spending more time in prayer will open your spiritual eye and the works of darkness can no longer be a pleasant practice any longer

> *John 1:9...that was the true Light, which lighteth every man that cometh into the world. KJV*

To empower means to give someone an official authority, or the freedom to do something. The freedom to destroy the works of darkness, which might be, making the wrong decision, walking in wrong assumption, harboring suspicious sentiments or the temptation to impatience and attack out of irritations. It is in prayer that one can access strong resisting power against the work of darkness, to destroy such attack and break such evil containers.

# Chapter 12

# WE PRAY TO OPEN PRISON DOORS FOR PEOPLE HELD BEHIND THEM

There is something special about praying for others. It is in praying for others that we see the power of the enemy weaken and finally made redundant in holding people in darkness. Many people want to serve God in Christ but are held continuously in evil patterns and evil circles. In the natural, people are locked up and contained in prison houses — some for short terms but others for life.

It's also same in the spirit. The whole world was placed under the sentence of death. Imprisoned and held by a wicked jailor, having no plans to let humanity free. In this state of affairs, satan also held gift, talent and all kinds of God given blessings in spiritual prisons. Then Jesus came in and paid the price for mankind by His sacrificial death. Men who believe can be made free and truly come into divine living with God.

The text below refers to the enemy as a jailor who has no intention of letting his prison free.

*Did he capture every city and make the earth a desert? Is he the one who refused to let prisoners go home?" CVE*

Violence, immorality, corruption, injustice, depression and oppression, to mention but a few are spiritual prisons the enemy still apply to people's lives. Keeping them contained in prisons where they cannot see the potentials locked up inside. They can only be set free by persistent prayer from others who are free. Just as there are legal processes and protocols involved in setting a prisoner free, praying is spiritual protocol. When a church prays, the people of the community will begin to experience greater levels of freedom. As sinners come in, deliverance will take place at ease for them. The local church that prays will enter into the abundance the Lord promised. (John 10:10)

*Pray and break them out from every demonic container.*

*Pray and break every evil container surrounding their calling today.*

*Pray and break every evil container surrounding their emotional growth today.*

*Pray and break every evil container surrounding your family lineage today.*

*Pray and Break every evil container surround your family's inheritance today.*

*Pray and break every evil container surrounding your unsaved children, wife, Husband today.*

*Pray and place a demand on the blood of Jesus as your legal ransom for release.*

*Pray and break their talent and gift from every circle of evil alliances, friends and fans.*

*Pray and break all break all chains holding back the arm of the Lord from your life in Jesus.*

# Chapter 13

# WE PRAY TO BUILD UP OUR SPIRITUAL RESERVES

"…Arise and eat for the journey is too great for you".

Too many people wait for moments of struggles and trials before thinking of their spiritual reserves. The car's fuel tank is designed with a special reserve marking. Whereby, each time we fill the tank, we fill on the reserve first before the excess is reached. Likewise, in prayer, we top up our spiritual reserve. You may have nothing to worry about or strive for at the moment, however, praying as a practice, is a means of filling your reserve just in the event of future occurrence.

The Cambridge dictionary defines to reserve as to keep something for a particular purpose or time. If one reserves something, it is for the purpose of using it in the future. So in prayer, we can build up spiritual reserve which we will end up needing someday. Prayer works that same way. Often when we pray, we may not be praying concerning what we need at the moment. This is the privilege we have as believers, we are giving the privilege to reserve spiritual favour in our live to be used in the future.

The principle in the text below will encourage you to pray even when you don't see manifestation. Reserve things in the cloud with your prayer, reserve seeds in the soil of your heart. Keep it very moist in prayer and you shall enjoy the fruit in times to come.

> *Ecclesiastes 11: 1Cast your bread upon the waters,*
> *for you will find it after many days.*
> *2 Give a portion to seven, or even to eight,*
> *for you know not what disaster may happen on earth.*
> *3 If the clouds are full of rain,*
> *they empty themselves on the earth,*
> *and if a tree falls to the south or to the north,*
> *in the place where the tree falls, there it will lie.*
> *4 He who observes the wind will not sow,*
> *and he who regards the clouds will not reap.*

There was a time a young lady shared her story with me. I listen in joy as she went on about how the Lord has blessed her and, in her mind, she could not remember when she had actually asked God in prayer for it. I shared with her that God is not a respecter of persons and that there is no blessing with an expectation or a request. In her time in prayer, she must have reserved her blessing and never knew it.

There was a time I came home after a journey and my wife pointed at a package and said "sweetheart this came in the post for you" and I could not remember when I ordered for it. God does not forget all we ask or think or imaging. He promised to answer and He will. The scripture says, He never forgets a labour of Love.

# PRAY POINT

- ➢ I thank you, for your power of remembrance.
- ➢ Your providence is working for me right now.
- ➢ Thank you, I receive the delivery of my portion.
- ➢ I break the seal and containers around all blessings with my name on it.

# Chapter 14

# WE PRAY TO BURN OUT THE FAT AND THE FLESH

To burn something is to be hurt, damaged, or destroyed it by fire or extreme heat. The flesh is in the New Testament carrying a more refined spiritual significance.

Leviticus 6:12...The fire on the altar is to be kept burning; it must not go out.

On the altars, oxen and other livestock will be sacrifice as an offering unto God by burning them to ash.

In the New Testament, the flesh refers to the carnal mind. A believer who still flirts with worldly ideologies and often agrees with it will be termed carnal and having a carnal mind.

> *Romans 8:5...For those who are according to the flesh and are controlled by its unholy desires set their minds on and pursue those things which gratify the flesh, but those who are according to the Spirit and are controlled*

*by the desires of the Spirit set their minds on and seek
those things which gratify the [Holy] Spirit.*

In this mindset, the individual will often, easily deviate from God's way of seeing and doing things to become motivated by the lust of life. The flesh is a power containing force that will drive a wedge between you and the Holy Spirit. You might be a professing Christian but the fruits, manifestation of the spirit will not become active in your life. It contains great a many gifting in the body of Christ from exploding in grace and power.

In prayer, we begin to hurt, damage or destroy such tendencies to over-rule our feelings and desires. Only in prayer, can we see more of who we are and the issues laying deep within our soul. The fat of the sacrifice was commanded by God to be placed on the alter and burned with fire.

Every morning, the priest will burn wood on the fire. He is to arrange the burnt offering on the fire and burn the fat portions from the fellowship offerings on it.

This alters in the new testaments is the alter of our heart in prayer.

> *Romans 12:11... Not slothful in business; <u>fervent in spirit</u>; serving the Lord; KJV*

Fervent conveys the attitude of being hot, being ablaze and burning with extreme passion for prayer and the word of God. The very understanding is to keep ablaze in the service of God. This is the place of fervent prayer where fat, flesh and carnality is extinguished.

*Acts 12:5...So indeed Peter was kept in the prison, but fervent prayer was being made to God by the church concerning him. BLB*

# Chapter 15

# WE PRAY TO CREATE THE ATMOSHPERE FOR MIRACLE

tmosphere is so key to how breakthroughs of blessings and miracles occur. There are many definitions that can be attached to the word atmosphere but these really blessed me; the air that you breathe in a place: it can also be referred to the character, feeling, or mood of a place or situation:

Miracles need certain atmosphere to really manifest. In the scripture, there was a blind man that Jesus had to lead out his village before He could begin the process of healing. It is obvious that Jesus needed a certain atmosphere for the miracle to manifest.

> *Mark 8:23...He took the blind man by the hand and led him outside the village. When he had spit on the man's eyes and put his hands on him, Jesus asked, "Do you see anything?"*

Prayer provokes such an atmosphere in houses, in churches and even in a whole region. In a cooperate worship setting, the atmosphere for the miraculous will always be experienced after a period of persistent prayers. In the book of Acts, often time, the place will be charged by the presence of God after a period of prayer.

> *Acts 2: 1- 4...And when the day of Pentecost was fully come, they were all with one accord in one place.[2] And suddenly there came a sound from heaven as of a rushing mighty wind, and it filled all the house where they were sitting. [3] And there appeared unto them cloven tongues like as of fire, and it sat upon each of them. [4] And they were all filled with the Holy Ghost, and began to speak with other tongues, as the Spirit gave them utterance.*

> *Acts 4:31... And when they had prayed, the place was shaken where they were assembled together; and they were all filled with the Holy Ghost, and they spake the word of God with boldness.*

At a certain time in the ministry of Paul, the Bible recorded several conflicts that Paul got caught in. In one of those conflicts, he was actually stoned to the point where they thought he was dead and left him as such. When the saint found his body, they made a circle around him, as it was creating an atmosphere for the miraculous, whereby, Paul had a supernatural recovery.

> *Acts 14:19-20... And there came thither certain Jews from Antioch and Iconium, who persuaded the people, and having stoned Paul, drew him out of the city, supposing he had been dead.[20] Howbeit, as the disciples*

*stood round about him, he rose up, and came into the city: and the next day he departed with Barnabas to Derbe.*

Prayer can transform any cold and stale place or situation into a vibrant spiritual atmosphere, allowing God to break forth and break out all containing factors. What happens in prayer causes a shift in atmosphere? Read on to the next sub chapter!

# Chapter 16

# WE PRAY TO RELEASE ANGELIC PARTICIPATION

There are certain dynamics which take place as the saints pray. In the book of revelation, it revealed how the prayer of the saint is mixed with incense which ascends on the altar by the hand of an angel.

> *Revelation 8:3-4...And another angel came and stood at the altar, having a golden censer; and there was given unto him much incense, that he should offer it with the prayers of all saints upon the golden altar which was before the throne. ⁴And the smoke of the incense, which came with the prayers of the saints, ascended up before God out of the angel's hand.*

Participation refers to you becoming involved in something, and taking your responsibility to ensure the success of a thing or project. Just as the book of Mark ended by saying ...Mark 16:²⁰ And they went forth, and preached everywhere, the Lord working with them, and confirming the word with signs following. Amen. KJV

Jesus participated through the Holy Spirit in their preaching and teaching the Word. So also, as we begin to pray, the atmosphere gets saturated with the miraculous, for angelic forces are drawn to the voices of prayer by the word of The Lord.

> *Daniel 10:12. "Do not be afraid, Daniel," he said, "for from the first day that you purposed to understand and to humble yourself before your God, your words were heard, and I have come in response to them BSB.*

This visitation presents a clear indication of angelic participation at the place of prayer. Daniel got a visit from angelic forces when he had set the atmosphere conducive enough. It is such an atmosphere that triggers the supernatural: The angelic realm is as real as the natural realms; they are highly active in service for the Lord. In the book of Psalms, it reveals, how angels excel in strength by the word of God.

> *Psalms 103:20...Bless the LORD, all his angels of great strength, who do his word, obedient to his command. CEV*

These are the instigators of the supernatural. They are responsible when the atmosphere starts changing and becoming conducive for the move of God. Praying is a fundamental key, if the church of God will move in greater power and vitality in the spirit.

Jesus could have provoked the angels into service to save Him in Gethsemane, when He reprimanded Peter to put away his sword; saying

*Matthew 26:53 ...Thinkest thou that I cannot now pray to my Father, and he shall presently give me more than twelve legions of angels? KJV*

As believers, we have inherited the same privileges in Christ; Conferring in essence, that angelic being align themselves whenever or wherever the word of God is being declared, especially on the subject of prayers.

*John 16:15 All things that the Father hath are mine: therefore said I, that he shall take of mine, and shall shew it unto you.*

# CHAPTER 17

# WE PRAY TO REMOVE DEMONIC VAILS AND COVERS

Covering refers to shielding something from something else. In the book of Ezekiel, we find that satan's major anointing is to cover. satan covers the world from the glorious gospel.

*Ezekiel 28:14. Thou art the anointed cherub that covereth; and I have set thee so: thou wast upon the holy mountain of God; thou hast walked up and down in the midst of the stones of fire.*

Which implies that after his rebellion, that the gift was not taking away.

There are certain layers that can mask and contain individuals in obscurity. Levels of mediocrity and unfruitfulness. Where they never seem to break that glass ceiling. He uses this skill to blind, deafens, and paralyzes the spiritual sense of humans. The word calls the enemy the god of this world who blinds individuals from coming to the light of the Gospel.

2 Corinthians 4:4... In whom the god of this world hath blinded the minds of them which believe not, lest the light of the glorious gospel of Christ, who is the image of God, should shine unto them.

During the transformation of Apostles Paul, it is on record how scales fell from his eye as soon as Ananias had ended laying hands on him. This scale signifies the darkness Paul was existing in. He persecuted and hauled many to prison for execution and imprisonment. He did all these, in his own words.

For we wrestle <u>not against flesh and blood</u>, but against principalities, against powers, against the rulers of the darkness of this world, against spiritual wickedness in high places...

Against men, who are of a frail and brittle nature, against whom are set spiritual wiles, a thousand times mightier than the natural. So It is imperative to become progressive in the knowledge of the demonic and its intent to cover and hinder people from the truth of God's words.

Acts 26: 9... I verily thought with myself, that I ought to do many things contrary to the name of Jesus of Nazareth.[10] Which thing I also did in Jerusalem: and many of the saints did I shut up in prison, having received authority from the chief priests; and when they were put to death, I gave my voice against them.[11] And I punished them oft in every synagogue, and compelled them to blaspheme; and being exceedingly mad against them, I persecuted them even unto strange cities. KJV

Apostle Paul was at this time of his life reflecting on his own actions. There were peculiar virtues in Paul, as the fact of keeping the law. He was morally sound, he did all in his strength to preserve the traditions past down by the fathers. He was zealous and passionate, a holy man according to God's law and very well educated in the Jewish faith, he was an outstanding figure among the leaders of his day.

However, his blindness to the essence of salvation found in God was great. Hence, he counted it but dung for the knowledge of the glory of God found in Christ.

Philippians 3:7-8...But Christ has shown me that what I once thought was valuable is worthless. [8]Nothing is as wonderful as knowing Christ Jesus my Lord. I have given up everything else and count it all as garbage. All I want is Christ CEV

# More Reasons to Pray!

WE PRAY BECAUSE THERE IS AN END TO ALL MATTER.
(1Peter 4:7) But the end of all things is at hand: be ye therefore sober, and watch unto prayer.
(Psalm 97:5) The hills melted like wax at the presence of the LORD, at the presence of the Lord of the whole earth. When God appears, to fulfil his promises and execute his threatenings, all opposition vanishes before him and all difficulties disappear. All difficulties vanished, all enemies were subdued, the gospel triumphed over all. The hills" symbolize the heights or man's self-exalting pride of intellect, wealth, and power. --A.R. Faussett.

WE PRAY BECAUSE WITH PRAYERS WE BREAK THE TEETH OF EVIL.
(Ps 58:6) Break their teeth, O God, in their mouth: break out the great teeth of the young lions, O LORD.
Teeth is a symbol of the powerful instrument the enemies possess to do mischief. It is a feature in mammals which contains deadly poison.
If they have no capacity for good, at least deprive them of their ability for evil. Treat the enemy as the snake charmers do their serpents, extract their fangs, and break their teeth.

WE PRAY TO DEPRIVE THE ENEMY OF THE ABILITY TO DO EVIL
(Ps 58:7) Let them melt away as waters which run continually: when he bendeth his bow to shoot his arrows, let them be as cut in pieces.
Let them be swept away like the waters which sometimes run in the desert, but are soon evaporated by the sun, or absorbed by the sand.

WE PRAY TO DRY UP THEIR EVIL WATERS
(Ps 58:7) Melt away-As waters arising from melted snow, which at first run with great force, but are suddenly gone.
So, pray to deal with and to take away all opportunities and means by which the enemy can hurt you.

49

PRAY "I DEPRIVE THE ENEMY'S
ABILITY TO INFLICT EVIL!

LET THE ENEMY'S ABILITY BE
WASTED IN ALL IT EFFORTS

IN THE NAME OF JESUS"

# BEWARE OF EVIL INTERACTIONS

# Chapter 18

# BEWARE OF EVIL INTERACTIONS

t this point, let's understand how mostly satan uses people. As much as we will like to believe that God uses people, in other to fulfil His will and counsel on the earth; satan employs the help of individuals to do likewise. People sometimes consciously or subconsciously will avail their soul and body to the enemy, so he can express his evil desires on earth.

Ephesians 4:19...who in time past have given themselves over unto lasciviousness, to work all uncleanness with greediness.

Acts 5:3-4...But Peter said, "Ananias, why has Satan filled your heart to lie to the Holy Spirit and to keep back for yourself part of the proceeds of the land? While it remained unsold, did it not remain your own? And after it was sold, was it not at your disposal? Why is it that you have contrived this deed in your heart? You have not lied to man but to God."

Luke 22;3...Then entered Satan into Judas surnamed Iscariot, being of the number of the twelve.

# Chapter 19

# THERE ARE DISCEPTIVE PEOPLE (AGAINST THE WILES OF THE DEVIL.)

The Cambridge dictionary defines deception to be a statement or action that hides the truth, or the act of hiding the truth:

Pray that God can cause you to be aware of deceptive people, who may intentionally hide the truth just to bring you into certain contempt; people whose aim is to mislead you with ulterior motives.

Beware of individuals who flow with others because of what they will enjoy from them. It is on your interest to pray for God to open your spiritual senses and to receive the gift of discernment in this season.

Jesus warns about the last hours before his coming, that "And many false prophets shall rise, and shall deceive many" (Matthew 24:11). Your prayer must include the place of being careful not to fall into the hand of deceptive people.

A prime example of a deceptive individual in the Bible was Ahithophel, whose name meant a brother of ruin and folly. His counsel was as the oracle of God. 2 Samuel 16:23...Ahithophel gave such good advice in those days that both Absalom and David thought it came straight from God.

2 Samuel 15:31...Someone told David, "Ahithophel is helping Absalom plot against you!" David said, "Please, LORD, keep Ahithophel's plans from working!"

Just like David prayed, this should be your prayers as well; All forms of deception from the enemy must fail in Jesus Name.

Other reference to study (1 Kings 13:11-32)

*Chapter 20*

# THERE ARE WICKED PEOPLE

*(Genesis 13:13) But the men of Sodom were wicked and sinners before the LORD exceedingly. (Psalm 7:9/ Ezekiel 18:20/ Ezekiel 33:12)*

The men of Sodom were wicked men. Another translation CEV, puts it this way, "where the people were evil and sinned terribly against the LORD".

Their wickedness grew to attract heaven's attention and judgment. Wickedness is the place where the human heart grows cold. Where humans are dehumanized in morality and evil practices, many may only have sexual immorality as the sin of Sodom. However, we read of gluttony, depriving the old and molesting the weak. It was a cut-throat society where everyone exploits.

Where there is wickedness, there is intense exploitation. Wicked people are at the end of all hoarding in society, they create a society of greed, starvation and shortages. Wicked people are war hungry because in it, is gain. Stay out of contention in order to resist the temptation to become part of the greed, scheming systems of this world.

Pray intensely against all wickedness scheduled by the enemy to disrupt God's plans for your life. There are people who live in severe wickedness of thought and evil and It is known of people who were hurt by people without reason.

# Chapter 21

# There are Possessed People

*(Mark 5:2) And when he was come out of the ship, immediately there met him out of the tombs a man with an unclean spirit.*

*(Acts 16:16) And it came to pass, as we went to prayer, a certain damsel possessed with a spirit of divination met us, which brought her masters much gain by soothsaying {of divination}.*

There are different levels of possession when it comes to the human race. There are demon-possessed individuals, who become host to evil spirits with the intension to carry out all kinds of disruption to human lives. They can inflict pain, orchestrate failure, misfortune, sicknesses, accidents, political unrest, regional unrest, racial unrests and any more chaotic socio-economic misfortune.

As a believer, it is very imperative to understand that your prayer will both expose these individuals and repel all spiritual attacks. The demon possessed in our text could not be stopped, not even by chains. However, he bowed before Jesus Christ.

Nothing will stop you in Jesus Name. The young girl was possessed with an evil spirit yet no one knew until Apostle Paul showed up. It takes prayer to expose deep seated evil in a region. The church in the region must establish the people in precision prayer to break evil spiritual containments.

# Chapter 22

# THERE ARE HATEFUL PEOPLE

*(John 15:19) If ye were of the world, the world would love his own: but because ye are not of the world, but I have chosen you out of the world, therefore the world hateth you.*

*(1John 3:13) Marvel not, my brethren, if the world hates you.*

Hate is a strong emotion, rooted in envy. Usually hateful people are led by a desire to Hatred people can ruin your life and turn the good things happening in your life to become evil. Most times hate may not be obvious.

They may come to you with smiles and even compliment but in their hearts, is a burning desire to see you fail. I pray you will persist in prayer and allow God to open your eye to these realities.

You may also want to pray for yourself at this point, because we can come to a place where we may be tempted to hate the other person for one reason or another. We are living in a world of many influences. You may have received false information on matter and may have come to a negative conclusion, which can spark off hatred. Pray against temptation.

## CONTENDING WITH HATEFULNESS

### THAT WE MAY NOT ENTER INTO TEMPTATION

*(Luke 22:40) And when he was at the place, he said unto them, Pray, that ye enter not into temptation.*

# Chapter 23

# THERE ARE IGNORANT PEOPLE

*(Ps 106:23) Therefore he said that he would destroy them, had not Moses his chosen stood before him in the breach, to turn away his wrath, lest he should destroy them. KVJ*

There is a time where we need to stand in for people. Most pain inflicted are due to the ignorance of people. People say and do things largely out of their ignorance. We must pray that these words we hear will not end up trapping our emotions and steal away our motivation.

Ignorance is a strong tool the enemy can use against relationships, business partners, students, the young, even the wise. In the scriptures the enemy is called, the prince of darkness — a term that points at his ability to keep one in the dark concerning specific issues.

The enemy can plant ignorant people within your organisation. They can become part of your board members, or part of your advisory team. The enemy can also motivate one by a moment of ignorance, where an individual will cause ruin or damage to a healthy project either by a wrong financially or spiritual decision.

Pray for discernment and allow the Holy Spirit to guide you at all times.

## PRAY FOR YOUR SPIRITUAL EYES TO BE OPEN

*Ephesians 1:18...The eyes of your understanding being enlightened; that ye may know what is the hope of his calling, and what the riches of the glory of his inheritance in the saints,*

# Chapter 24

# THERE ARE EVIL PEOPLE

*(2 Kings 8:18) And he walked in the way of the kings of Israel, as did the house of Ahab: for the daughter of Ahab was his wife: and he did evil in the sight of the LORD.*

*(2 Kings 8:26-27) Two and twenty years old was Ahaziah when he began to reign; and he reigned one year in Jerusalem. And his mother's name was Athaliah, the daughter of Omri king of Israel. And he walked in the way of the house of Ahab, and did evil in the sight of the LORD, as did the house of Ahab: for he was the son in law of the house of Ahab*

Is hate a right emotion to feel when it comes to evil tendency and action in people's lives? Below are the words of Christ.

*(Revelation 2:6) But this thou hast, that thou hatest the deeds of the Nicolaitans, **which I also hate.***

The Greek word for **Hate** is miseo - to hate, to abhor, or to find utterly repulsive. The term describes someone with deep seated animosity... a person who is antagonistic, who finds something completely objectionable.

Evil people are profoundly immoral and wicked in thought and deeds. The word warns us to beware of evil communications because they ruin manners.

> *1 Corinthians 15:33..Be not deceived: evil communications corrupt good manners.*

At certain times in your life, there is need for a line to be drawn from individual who blatantly engages in behaviors and lifestyle contrary to scripture. We see an escalation of Christians who find it usual to live certain immoral and evil lifestyle. It isn't right to indulge in such and we can be drawn into thinking it is, simply because we have not seen any visible sign of judgment by God. God is merciful but satan is not. Satan keeps such motives alive by deception while leading others astray due to their evil concupiscence.

These are people who urge and resist the word of God from taking roots in their hearts. They to stand against the counsel of God and take divine matter lightly. In these last days, prepare yourselves against such people. They will resist and stand against you simple because of what you believe or the issues stand for. Rest assured, they will fall in the face of Jesus Christ.

> *2 Thessalonians 3:1...Finally, brethren, pray for us, that the word of the Lord may have free course, and be glorified, even as it is with you*

*(Ac 4:26) The kings of the earth stood up, and the rulers were gathered together against the Lord, and against his Christ.*

# Chapter 25

# THERE ARE FALSE BRETHREN TO UNCOVER

*(1John 2:18) Little children, it is the last time: and as ye have heard that antichrist shall come, even now are there many antichrists; whereby we know that it is the last time. 19 <u>They went out from us,</u> but they were not of us; for if they had been of us, they would no doubt have continued with us: but they went out, that they might be made manifest that they were not all of us. KJV*

In the book of Revelation there are false brethren like Balaam and Nicolas the deacon.

*(The Nicolaitans revelation 2:6... but there is one thing you are doing right. You hate what the Nicolaitans are doing, and so do I)*

Ireneus and Hippolytus, early church fathers who chronicled many of the earliest events in church history, have recorded that the Nicolaitans were spiritual descendants of Nicolas the Deacon. History reports that Nicolas was one of the deacons who was ordained in the book of Act 6:5. He was a Proselyte Jew – which meant he was a convert to Judaism. It was told, before his conversion, he was a pagan and practiced paganism. Usually such individuals would be dedicated occult practitioners.

According to records, when he heard the message of salvation from God through Jesus Christ, Nicolas gladly embraced it. In the book of Acts, he was mentioned among the men that were of good report, full of the Holy Ghost and wisdom.

Acts 6:3... Wherefore, brethren, look ye out among you seven **men of** honest report, **full of** the Holy Ghost and **wisdom**, whom we may appoint over this business.

Yet, the deep root of paganism still existed in him and true conversion had not taken roots. Thence, he began teaching a gospel of compromise - which corresponded with his liberal nature. Nicolas saw nothing wrong in serving God through Jesus and also indulging in idolatry, witchcraft and mysticism.

False brethren may not be as extreme as Nicolas however if individuals do not esteem the integrity of the word of God over certain behaviour and lifestyle then very soon the tendency to flow into false worship will be greater.

# PRAYER VERSES

*2Cor. 11:26…During my many travels, I have been in danger from rivers, robbers, my own people, and foreigners. My life has been in danger in cities, in deserts, at sea, and with people who only pretended to be the Lord's followers.*

*Psalms 119:105…Thy word is a lamp unto my feet, and a light unto my path.*

# PRECISION PRAYERS

This section is designed with the reader in mind, in other to ensure a delightful time in praying. Every sentence, bullet point and scripture, opens a portal for engagement.

# DESTRUCTION OF THE SPIRIT OF SEGREGATION

REFERENCE: The wall of Jericho… spirit of contamination … spirit on Naaman

## SPIRIT OF SEGREGATION.

Joshus6:1…Now Jericho was straitly shut up because of the children of Israel: none went out, and none came in. Segregation means the deliberate detachment of two or more groups! By this spirit the enemy will create many false images that lead to failure! For instance, the enemy…

- Diminishes the value of something (Human value: Value of perspective … when someone devalues the worth of something (i.e. Take a nice outfit or evening wear and wear for work at a construction site) Spiritual value (hides people's spiritual worth both theirs and the value of others?),
- Creates a lie of position, (i.e. You actually have a false perspective either low or high
- Removes the energy of creativity which is unity,

- Breaks down marriages and homes
- Kills talents
- Create misleading paths
- Strategizes to separate for the kill.
- Separates potential from potency **in the soul...** (potency is what makes potential latent Work Gives it power and that spirit separates It separates dreams from reality
- Prevents the mind and body from walking in union
- Creates division between friends, family and church
- Stimulates a proud look
- Causes one to look down on another.

# Chapter 27

# SPIRIT OF CONTAMINATION

*(2Ki 5:1) Now Naaman, captain of the host of the king of Syria, was a great man with his master, and honourable, because by him the LORD had given deliverance unto Syria: he was also a mighty man in valour, but he was a leper.*

- This is a spirit of disgrace.
- It embarrasses an individual, a family or even business.
- It has a dimension that makes a good deed look bad,
- Turns a talented person into a person with an addiction or an attitude problem.
- It amplifies one's past weaknesses
- Its intention is to undermine a person's progress
- Though you may be great it will try to show your failures to the world
- It tries to reduce your testimony
- It uses the "buts" to cripple the "nevertheless"
- It tries to bring into one's life a lone life

# Chapter 28

# Destruction of Spirit of Violence

*(Mark 5:4) Because that he had been often bound with fetters and chains, and the chains had been plucked asunder by him, and the fetters broken in pieces: neither could any man tame him. 5 And always, night and day, he was in the mountains, and in the tombs, crying, and cutting himself with stone*

*(Ps 18:13) The LORD also thundered in the heavens, and the Highest gave his voice; hail stones and coals of fire.*

*(Ps 21:9) Thou shalt make them as a fiery oven in the time of thine anger: the LORD shall swallow them up in his wrath, and the fire shall devour them.*

iolence can be described in various terms, but in our study, we will describe as dictionary.com states it, "rough or injurious physical, action or treatment"

So, violence is a forceful act or behavior involving physical force with the intention to hurt, damage or kill.

In the realms of the spirit, this is a demon-spirit of aggression… a spirit that intimidates and takes possession of people's lives. It can be passive aggression or active aggression. These are aggressive voices, speaking with elevated treats against movements to the progress of any sort.

Goliath is a type of this violent voice in the book of 1 Samuel 17:8 Goliath went out and shouted to the army of Israel: CVE . The NLT gave, he stood and shouted a taunt across to the Israelites.

- It enforces hatred among people either from other or what is known as self-hatred. Where individuals become their number critic, they end up being tired of themselves by becoming increasingly critical of themselves for wrong doing, failures, and wrong judgments. You got to stand against this containing spirit by the word of God in prayer.
- It is behind all forms of anger and the promotion of anger. Do you suffer from uncontrollable anger, where irritation gets the best of you? Then this spirit is in operation. It comes in to justify anger. Some individuals have attained some result using the resource of anger to work things into their favour but it will soon catch up. Anger will eventually tie it host down. It is a powerful containing strategy of the enemy.
- It is the enforcer of rebellion against a blessed life. This spirit cannot stand the presence of the blessing. It gets irritable where good testimonies are being read. It becomes rebellious in the face of possible change and advancement.
- It carries out all forms of intimidating processes (Eze. 28:16). By the multitude of thy merchandise, they have filled the

midst of thee with violence, and thou hast sinned: therefore I will cast thee as profane out of the mountain of God: and I will destroy thee, O covering cherub, from the midst of the stones of fire.

- It prevents the fulfilment of wealth and riches (Psalm 112:3...) Wealth and riches shall be in his house: and his righteousness endureth forever. Wealth and riches are not for fool, as the bible says through wisdom a house is built but anger rest in the bossom of fool. Ecclesiastes 7:9...Do not hasten in your spirit to be angry, For anger rests in the bosom of fools. KJV
- It causes deep emotional hurt (instability of decisions)
- It makes one to go out of control (that is his plan to make one lose their destiny)
- It tries forcefully to bind the eye of Purpose
- It knows no law, and is against healthy restriction.
- It provokes a waste of resources.
- It fights against good counsel (Proverb 24:6)
- This spirit is behind all terrorism and violence. (Jer. 51:46) And lest your heart faint, and ye fear for the rumour that shall be heard in the land; a rumour shall both come one year, and after that in another year shall come a rumour, and violence in the land, ruler against ruler.
- This spirit is involved in starting strife in a church (Ps 55:9) Destroy, O Lord, and divide their tongues: for I have seen violence and strife in the city.

# PRAYER POINT

➤ (Ps 68:30) Rebuke the company of spearmen, the multitude of the bulls, with the calves of the people, till every one submit himself with pieces of silver: scatter thou the people that delight in war.

# Chapter 29

# SPIRIT OF IGNORANCE

*Isaiah 56:10 His watchmen are blind: **they are all ignorant**, they are all dumb dogs, they cannot bark; sleeping, lying down, loving to slumber*

Ignorance means the lack of knowledge, information or education. In prayer ignorance is a lack of revelation, which means one may not believe will be attacked by an inability to comprehend the voice of the Spirit, either in worship or in word of God. This situation can lead to series of misguided decisions and assumptions.

The spirit of ignorance can

- Prevents proper worship
- Covers the light of the word
- Makes people to apply the word wrongly
- Its desire is to mislead in spiritual things
- Prevents one from using spiritual gifts
- Releases ignorance to cover access to the 7 spirits of God

- Lies about the love of God
- Tries to take over the mouth of positive confession
- Breaks the understanding process
- Hides the effort others are making
- Estranges people from healthy relationships
- Prevents the flow of love in a church

- Is the bringer of envy, hate, negative competition and mischievous act

# PRAYER POINTS

- ➢ I resist the powers of Darkness to rule over my mind. I declare that I walk because God has brought into his light.
- ➢ 1 Peter 2:9…But ye *are* a chosen generation, a royal priesthood, a holy nation, a peculiar people; that ye should shew forth the praises of him who hath called you out of darkness into his marvellous light:
- ➢ 1 Corinthians 2:16…For who hath known the mind of the Lord, that he may instruct him? But we have the mind of Christ.

# Chapter 30

# DESTRUCTION OF THE SPIRIT OF EVIL

The spirit of evil is an inventive spirit. It is a known fact that satan cannot create anything, yet scripture tells us in Romans 1:29: Being filled with all unrighteousness, fornication, wickedness, covetousness, maliciousness; full of envy, murder, debate, deceit, malignity; whisperers, 30... Backbiters, haters of God, despiteful, proud, boasters, **inventors of evil things**, disobedient to parent ...

Therefore, in the world of darkness there are things that will come forward and one will (cannot help but) wonder "where did that come from" ... like the laws being considered in some countries in areas of sexuality, addictive substances, alcohol and medical science to mention but a few.

# INVENTORS OF EVIL THINGS

**(Evil words, evil thoughts, evil intentions, evil look, evil instructions, evil counsel**

- This spirit of evil conjures up evil ideas
- It makes right look wrong and wrong look right
- It creates areas for the promotion of evil
- It uses unrepented images of the mind (this is a good reason why we need to purge our minds)
- It causes the desire of evil to materialize
- It carries out a distortion of emotion
- It allows unforgiveness to fester long enough for the destructive power of revenge to manifest)

- This will try to bring counsel intended for evil

## PRAYER POINT

➢ (2 Samuel 15:31).And one told David, saying, Ahithophel is among the conspirators with Absalom. And David said, O LORD, I pray thee, turn the counsel of Ahithophel into foolishness.

# Chapter 31

# DESTRUCTION OF SPIRIT OF INFIRMITY

*(Luke 13:10) And he was teaching in one of the synagogues on the sabbath.11 And, behold, there was a woman which had a spirit of infirmity eighteen years, and was bowed together, and co<u>uld in no wise lift up</u> <u>herself:12 And when Jesus saw her, he called her to</u> <u>him, and said unto her, Woman, thou art loosed from</u> <u>thine infirmity. And he laid his hands on her: and</u> <u>immediately she was made straight, and glorified God.</u>*

**I**nfirmity means feebleness (of mind or body) from the root word **strengthless** or being without strength, weak, sick or impotent.

The spirit of infirmity:

- Is the causer of many diseases
- Is the preventer of healing
- Is the holder of diseases by causing weakness and feebleness to fight

- Is the causer of various types of dissatisfaction and frustrations of the heart
- Is the introduces to the realms of the spirit past sins
- Is the door-opener of generational curses, and that which makes the curses to stick (proverbs 26:2) as the bird by wandering, as the swallow by flying, **so the curse causeless shall not come.**
- Is the spirit that tries to break the physical body with continuous sicknesses
- Is the spirit that frustrates prayer and fasting
- Is the spirit that lies about present conditions of the body and mind – lying to it about a state of weakness
- Is the spirit that relates to the soul the lie that there is no hope
- Is the unseen burden that ends up pressing individuals in life (luke 13:11) and, behold, there was a woman which had a spirit of infirmity eighteen years, and was bowed together, and could in no wise lift up herself.
- Ultimately wants to bring shame on god's promise (luke 13:16) and ought not this woman, being a daughter of abraham, whom satan hath bound, lo, these eighteen years, be loosed from this bond on the sabbath day?17 and when he had said these things, **all his adversaries were ashamed**: and all the people rejoiced for all the glorious things that were done by him.
- Is the enforcer of barrenness. Infirmity also means impotent!

# PRAYER POINTS

- (Proverbs 20:8...A king that sitteth in the throne of judgment scattereth away all evil with his eyes.
- Psalms 68:1...Let God arise, let his enemies be scattered: let them also that hate him flee before him.
- Psalms 27:1...The LORD is my light and my salvation; whom shall I fear? the LORD is the strength of my life; of whom shall I be afraid?
- Psalms 103:3...Who forgiveth all thine iniquities; who healeth all thy diseases;

# Chapter 32

# DESTRUCTION OF SPIRIT OF DEATH AND HELL

*(1Corinthians 15:26) The last enemy that shall be destroyed is death.*

*(Revelation 20:14) And death and hell were cast into the lake of fire. This is the second death.*

*(1 Corinthians 15:55) O death, where is thy sting? O grave, where is thy victory? {grave or hell}*

The major assignment of the spirit of death and Hell is to break down divine connection and communication in the spirit. Its work is to dampen the move of the spirit in a church or community to eventually silence the voice of prophesy in the earth.

These spirits (death and Hell) work as a team… as a partner to ensure that satan finishes his assignment of stealing, killing and destroying. After all tricks and schemes, satan, unleashes this spirit to attack and dissolve God's ultimate plan in your life. This spirit is responsible in the break-down of families and the separation of children from parents. They instigate and launch these attacks in all realms; spiritually, psychologically, physically and financially.

This spirit intends to:

- Quenches the spirit (1Thessalonians 5:19) Quench not the Spirit
- Quenches the prayer of faith. (James 5:15) And the prayer of faith shall save the sick, and the Lord shall raise him up; and if he has committed sins, they shall be forgiven him.
- Tries to quench the voice of prophecy (1Thessalonians 5:20) Despise not prophesying. Where there is no prophecy there will be no life...
- (1Co 14:3) But he that prophesieth speaketh unto men to edification, and exhortation, and comfort.:4 He that speaketh in an unknown tongue edifieth himself; but he that prophesieth edifieth the church :5 I would that ye all spake with tongues, but rather that ye prophesied: for greater is he that prophesieth than he that speaketh with tongues, except he interpret, that the church may receive edifying Why because their life in your tongue...
- Attempts to Quench the life of fasting and prayer (Mark 9:29) And he said unto them, This kind can come forth by nothing, but by prayer and fasting.

- ✓ Fasting and prayer are combined forces that release spiritual forces
- ✓ When we fast we release the power in our spirit to take over our soul and body
- ✓ When we fast and pray we distribute the power of the spirit to the areas we need it most
- ✓ When we fast and pray our eyes open to new truths that were not seen before
- ✓ When we fast we take to a new dimension in the spirit
- ✓ When we fast and pray power is delivered for effectiveness in our giving assignment
- ✓ When we fast and pray, we take off the slumber of the spirit, soul and body
- ✓ When we fast and pray we submit easily to the plans of God
- ✓ when we fast and pray our hearts to break-off containments
- ✓ when we fast and pray things that look impossible to begin to change
- ✓ when we fast and pray we switch to a different perspective in life
- ✓ when we fast and pray we expand our territory in the spirit realms
- ✓ when we fast and pray burdens are lifted off our live, and the lives of others
- ✓ when we fast and pray we declare our reliance on God and His kingdom for our supplies
- ✓ When we fast and pray. Our health will be restored

In other words Fasting and Prayers should never cease. When they do, death comes in.

- It attempts to quench the vibrancy of the spirit
- Causes untimely death - both Physically and spiritually. (Exodus 12:29) And it came to pass, that at midnight the LORD smote all the firstborn in the land of Egypt, from the firstborn of Pharaoh that sat on his throne unto the firstborn of the captive that was in the dungeon; and all the firstborn of cattle.
    - Before this event God told Moses that the destroyer would be released (Exodus 12:23) For the LORD will pass through to smite the Egyptians; and when he seeth the blood upon the lintel, and on the two side posts, the LORD will pass over the door, and will not suffer the destroyer to come in unto your houses to smite you.
    - Presses Down to destroy on the spring of new life ...Song 2:15 Take us the foxes, the little foxes, that spoil the vines: for our vines have tender grapes
    - Whenever anything new is rising a new star to shine in people's lives, a new voice, a new gifting, a new marriage, a new vision, this FOX springs in to cause sudden death.
    - This spirit can also be referred to as the <u>spirit of the fox Luke 13:32</u>, <u>the spirit of Pharoah</u>, <u>the spirit of Herod...</u> All these are entities that propagated sudden death to new voices

# PEOPLES UNDER THE INFLUENCE OF THE SPIRIT OF DEATH AND HELL

| | |
|---|---|
| **Pharoah** | Pharoah ordered the killing of Children but Moses escaped (Exodus 1:22) And Pharaoh charged all his people, saying, Every son that is born ye shall cast into the river, and every daughter ye shall save alive<br><br>Hence Moses' name means Drawn out! The daughter of Pharoah said "I drew him out of the water" |
| **The 1ˢᵗ Herod** | 1ˢᵗ: Herod the great (Mathew 2:16) Then Herod, when he saw that he was mocked of the wise men, was exceeding wroth, and sent forth, and slew all the children that were in Bethlehem, and in all the coasts thereof, from two years old and under, according to the time which he had diligently enquired of the wise men. Because in verse 13 the angel had warned Joseph in a dream to take Jesus and Mary to Egypt until Herod's death. (Matthew 2:15) And was there until the death of Herod: that it might be fulfilled which was spoken of the Lord by the prophet, saying, Out of Egypt have I called my son.<br><br>This Herod, though a skilled politician, was a ruthless and brutal man who killed his father in-law, several of his ten wives, and two of his sons. He ignored God's laws to suit himself and chose the favor of Rome over his own people. |
| **The 2ⁿᵈ Herod** | The 2ⁿᵈ: Herod, Herod's son Archelaus, killed 3000 men in the temple in one evening – for no other reason but for power. Jesus referred to him in (Luke 13:31) The same day there came certain of the Pharisees, saying unto him, Get thee out, and depart hence: for Herod will kill thee :32… And he said unto them, Go ye, and tell **that fox**, Behold, I cast out devils, and I do cures today and tomorrow, and the third day I shall be perfected. |

# Chapter 33

# (JOHN 5:1-8)
# SPIRIT OF DEPRESSION

Depression being a spirit is concretely defined as grief: - heaviness, sorrow. In Psychiatry, it is known as a condition of general emotional dejection and withdrawal; sadness greater and more prolonged than that warranted by any objective reason.

Therefore there will be a persistent sadness, gloom, and the feeling of dejection.

This spirit…

- Is the generator of complaints (Job 9:27) If I say, I will forget my complaint, I will leave off my heaviness, and comfort myself:
- Is the generator of self-pity (Psalm 69:20) Reproach hath broken my heart; and I am full of heaviness: and I looked for some to take pity, but there was none; and for comforters, but I found none.

- Is the bringer of loneliness (Ps 119:28) My soul melteth for heaviness: strengthen thou me according unto thy word... because of overwhelming load of my afflictions causes my life to ebb and leak out as though God is not with us.. those times we cry and wonder God is there trying to strengthen us with His word

- Is the obstructer of God's project (Proverbs 24:3) Through wisdom is a house builded; and by understanding it is established:- in construction Depression means a sunken place, a defaulted area of a house/ a place being cracked

- Tries to attack the pure heart (Psalm 24:4) He that hath clean hands, and a pure heart; who hath not lifted up his soul unto vanity, nor sworn deceitfully :5 He shall receive the blessing from the LORD, and righteousness from the God of his salvation.

- This spirit is the father of Rejection

The pure heart God needs to bring forth the blessing (the pure heart, runs after God with all confidence... the pure heart renders worship and praise). But the pure in heart, can be attacked by depression. The spirit of depression can take over the mind with voices like "see, God has rejected you." Depression will even make matters arise which will give the impression, God has lost the battle. It will cause a pure hearted individual to begin to doubt and bow down to complain and rejection. It will do all it can to take away the individual from the confidence they have found in God and His Word. Stand strong it is not over yet until you win.

*(Ps 69:20) Reproach hath broken my heart; and I am full of heaviness: and I looked for some to take pity, but there was none; and for comforters, but I found none.*

*(John 5:7) The impotent man answered him, Sir, I have no man, when the water is troubled, to put me into the pool: but while I am coming, another steppeth down before me.*

*(Psalm 121) I will lift up mine eyes unto the hills, from whence cometh my help. {I will...: or, Shall I lift up mine eyes to the hills? whence should my help come?} 2 My help cometh from the LORD, which made heaven and earth.*

- The spirit of Depression will attempt to turn all your laughter to sorrow (Proverb 14:13) Even in laughter the heart is sorrowful; and the end of that process is heaviness.

- (Isa 61:3) To appoint unto them that mourn in Zion, to give unto them beauty for ashes, the oil of joy for mourning, the garment of praise for the spirit of heaviness; that they might be called trees of righteousness, the planting of the LORD, that he might be glorified.

In the bible, word depression is not used except in the new living translation. It uses the word downcast, sad, forlorn, discouraged, downhearted, mourning, troubled, miserable, despair and broken hearted, heaviness.

# PEOPLE WHO SUFFERED BRIEFLY
# FROM DEPRESSION

| | |
|---|---|
| **Hagar** | Hagar...Gen 21:16 And she went, and sat her down over against him a good way off, as it were a bowshot: for she said, Let me not see the death of the child. And she sat over against him, and lift up her voice, and wept. |
| **Joshua** | Joshua (Jos 1:6) Be strong and of a good courage: for unto this people shalt thou divide for an inheritance the land, which I swear unto their fathers to give them<br><br>Again God came and said the same thing...<br>(Joshua 1:7) Only be thou strong and very courageous, that thou mayest observe to do according to all the law, which Moses my servant commanded thee: turn not from it to the right hand or to the left, that thou mayest prosper whithersoever<br><br>On the third occasion... hear the tone<br><br>(Joshua 1:9) **Have not I commanded thee**? Be strong and of a good courage; be not afraid, neither be thou dismayed: for the LORD thy God is with thee whithersoever thou goest. |
| **Naomi** | **Naomi.** (Ruth 1:20) And she said unto them, Call me not Naomi, call me Mara: for the Almighty hath dealt very bitterly with me. {Naomi: that is, Pleasant} {Mara: that is, Bitter} |
| **Hannah** | **Hannah** (1Samuel 1:8) Then said Elkanah her husband to her, Hannah, why weepest thou? and why eatest thou not? and why is thy heart grieved? am not I better to thee than ten sons? |
| **David** | **David** (Psalm 69:20) Reproach hath broken my heart; and I am full of heaviness: |

| | |
|---|---|
| **Elijah** | **Elijah** (1King 19:10) And he said, I have been very jealous for the LORD God of hosts: for the children of Israel have forsaken thy covenant, thrown down thine altars, and slain thy prophets with the sword; and I, even I only, am left; and they seek my life, to take it away. |
| **Nehemiah** | **Nehemiah** (Nehemiah 1:4) And it came to pass, when I heard these words, that I sat down and wept, and mourned certain days, and fasted, and prayed before the God of heaven |
| **Job** | **Job** (Job 10:19) I should have been as though I had not been; I should have been carried from the womb to the grave. |
| **Jeremiah** | Jeremiah 20:14 – 18... Put a curse on the day I was born!<br>    Don't bless my mother.<br>15 Put a curse on the man<br>who told my father,<br>"Good news!<br>    You have a son."<br>16 May that man be like the towns<br>    you destroyed without pity.<br>Let him hear shouts of alarm<br>in the morning<br>    and battle cries at noon.<br>17 He deserves to die<br>for not killing me<br>    before I was born.<br>Then my mother's body<br>    would have been my grave.<br>18 Why did I have to be born?<br>Was it just to suffer<br>    and die in shame? |
| **Paul** | **Paul**<br>Roman 9:2...That I have great heaviness and continual sorrow in my heart. |
| **JESUS** | Isaiah 53:3...He is despised and rejected of men; a man of sorrows, and acquainted with grief: and we hid as it were *our* faces from him; he was despised, and we esteemed him not. |

# PRAYER POINT

I receive the love of the father; I am open for the love of God to rest me at this moment. I trust the Holy Spirit's comfort and direction. Lord, not my will but your will be done!

*Chapter 34*

# SPIRIT OF SICKNESSES AND DISEASE

*(Luke 8:43) And a woman having an issue of blood twelve years, which had spent all her living upon physicians, neither could be healed of any,*

This spirit, although it is the fruit of Infirmity, is a prevalent spirit with reproductive powers. By the tongue, this spirit can have a door into lives to cause destruction. The tongue is a powerful weapon and can be a channel by which powers are released to change the cause of people's lives. Words are conveyors of power and authority (proverb 18:21). When words are utter it invokes all forces to align with what you have spoken.

Interesting enough, many use words like "you make me feel sick" "that song is sick!" "I am going to sick as a dog". They make claims to certain sickness and are not aware of what is taking place in their world. Claims such as "this <u>my</u> headache always come back this time of the year" "I am used to this my sickness - I always had it"

This spirit of sickness and disease comes upon people (Exodus 15:26) And said, If thou wilt diligently hearken to the voice of the LORD thy God, and wilt do that which is right in his sight, and wilt give ear to his commandments, and keep all his statutes, I will put none of these diseases upon thee, which I have brought upon the Egyptians: for I am the LORD that healeth thee…

It must be recognized the first minute it touches your realms and refuses entry by your prayers and resistance to accept anything else order than sound health.

The spirit of sickness and disease can be referred to as the pestilence that walketh in darkness (Psalm 91:6) Nor for the pestilence that walketh in darkness; nor for the destruction that wasteth at noonday. (7) A thousand shall fall at thy side, and ten thousand at thy right hand; but it shall not come nigh thee.

The spirit of sickness and disease is a spirit that walks around, unseen by the eyes of men. It hides in the houses of people in order to place diseases and all sorts of illnesses on members of a family.

The spirit of sickness and disease will play a major role in the last days at the coming of Christ (Mathew 24:6) And ye shall hear of wars and rumours of wars: see that ye be not troubled: for all these things must come to pass, but the end is not yet. 7 For nation shall rise against nation, and kingdom against kingdom: and there shall be famines, and pestilences, and earthquakes, in divers places.

The spirit of sickness and disease carries the same dimension as the spirit of contamination, except that it can persist and mutate. But it can be cursed to disappear or depart in Jesus Name.

# THE SPIRIT OF SICKNESS AND DISEASE CAN BE CURSED TO DISAPPEAR OR DEPART

*(John 4:52) Then enquired he of them the hour when he began to amend. And they said unto him, Yesterday at the seventh hour the fever left him. (KJV)*

*(Mark 1:42) And as soon as he had spoken, immediately the leprosy departed from him, and he was cleansed.*

*(Luke 5:13) And he put forth his hand, and touched him, saying, I will: be thou clean. And immediately the leprosy departed from him.*

therapeuo, ther-ap-yoo'-o …to relieve (of disease):--cure, heal, worship.

*(Mathew 4:23) And Jesus went about all Galilee, teaching in their synagogues, and preaching the gospel of the kingdom, and healing all manner of sickness and all manner of disease among the people.*

therapeuo, ther-ap-yoo'-o …to relieve (of disease):-cure, heal, worship)

Cure means to make well again/ to put an end to (a disease, a condition or problem) by treatment… by appropriate action.

Heal means to make or become sound again, or become well.

The spirit of sickness and disease appoints or assigns "the destroyer". It cuts lives short or brings sudden death.

The spirit of sickness and disease attacks family structure. When you hear things like "this sickness is genetic or hereditary", this lie has claimed the lives of so many loved ones.

The spirit of sickness and disease destroys wealth (Job 15:21) A dreadful sound is in his ears: in prosperity the destroyer shall come upon him.

The aim of the spirit of sickness and disease is to limit God's purpose by harvesting one's body from the earth before the appointed time. The revelation of living long is God's plan for extending one's life on the earth. That way one can be of greater service for Him. He wants us to live long and strong, in other to bring a lasting impact in the lives of the upcoming generation.

## PRAYER POINT

"Blessed Lord, take us into thy protection this night; and preserve us from disease, from sudden death, from the violence of fire, from the edge of the sword, from the designs of wicked men, and from the influence of malicious spirits!"

➤ (Psalm 121:5) The LORD is thy keeper: the LORD is thy shade upon thy right hand.

But The Lord will keep His own.
Every sudden death is rebuked in my family.
I refuse this spirit to operate in my world.
I call wholeness to my spirit, soul and body.

# Chapter 35

# DESTRUCTION OF SPIRIT OF PRIDE

*(1John 2:16) For all that is in the world, the lust of the flesh, and the lust of the eyes, and the pride of life, is not of the Father, but is of the world.*

ride is defined as being boastful. Another word for pride in the bible is Haughty… a haughty spirit. Although the use of pride can be on the positive, we are using this context from bible's perspective. From the third definition in the Collins English dictionary it defines pride, to someone feeling that they have that they are better or more important than other people. The scripture says (Pro 16:18) Pride goeth before destruction, and a haughty spirit before a fall.

- The Spirit of pride is the ruler of men /the nature of the devil
- The spirit of pride is the killer of the strongest and it disgraces those who become wise in their ways
- The spirit of pride is the nation's inspirer

- The spirit of pride is the producer of false identity
- The spirit of pride strangles with the God Image
- The spirit of pride is the burial ground of the elites
- The spirit of pride is the path maker to the cliff of surprise and misfortune
- The spirit of pride is the evil that filled satan
- The spirit of pride stimulates the tyrant and heartless to more folly. (Proverbs 21:24) Proud and haughty scorner is his name, who dealeth in proud wrath.
- The spirit of pride is the forerunner of failure
- The spirit of pride is among one of the spirits that make up the trinity of man
- The spirit of pride tries to hide the purpose of God

God's goal is to hide men from the lure of pride (Job 33:15) In a dream, in a vision of the night, when deep sleep falleth upon men, in slumberings upon the bed; 16 Then he openeth the ears of men, and sealeth their instruction, {he...: Heb. he revealeth, or, uncovereth} 17 That he may withdraw man from his purpose, and hide pride from man. {purpose: Heb. work}

# THE NATURE AND OPERARATION OF THE SPIRIT OF PRIDE

- The spirit of Pride is released to compete with God's reign
- The spirit of Pride is released with the deadly intent of replacing the plans of God (Ecclesiastes 7:8) Better is the end of a thing than the beginning thereof: and the patient in spirit is better than the proud in spirit. (Proverb 18:12) Before destruction the heart of man is haughty, and before honour is humility.

- The spirit of Pride intends to turn hearts from the worship of God to the worship of achievement (Acts 7:41) And they made a calf in those days, and offered a sacrifice unto the idol, and rejoiced in the works of their own hands

- The spirit of Pride fights within the heart of man to take the place of God, and the work of Jesus. Which induce men to save their lives, which we know it is just impossible to attain (1Samuel 2:9) He will keep the feet of his saints, and the wicked shall be silent in darkness; for by strength shall no man prevail.

- The spirit of Pride's intent is to introduce a counterfeit anointing (Jeremiah 43:2) Then spake Azariah the son of Hoshaiah, and Johanan the son of Kareah, and all the proud men, saying unto Jeremiah, Thou speakest falsely: the LORD our God hath not sent thee to say, Go not into Egypt to sojourn there. (Jeremiah 28:15) Then said the prophet Jeremiah unto Hananiah the prophet, Hear now, Hananiah; The LORD hath not sent thee; but thou makest this people to trust in a lie16... Therefore thus saith the LORD; Behold, I will cast thee from off the face of the earth: this year thou shalt die, because thou hast taught rebellion against the LORD. {rebellion: Heb. Revolt} 17...So Hananiah the prophet died the same year in the seventh month.

- The spirit of Pride intends to shift the believer from the anointing of God to the wisdom of men (1Corinthians 2:5) That your faith should not stand in the wisdom of men, **but in the power of God**.

Scripture calls
  - A proud look Proverb 6:17...A proud look, a lying tongue, and hands that shed innocent blood .

- o high mindedness. 2Timothy 3:4...Traitors, heady, high-minded, lovers of pleasures more than lovers of God. (self-conceit:--high-minded, be lifted up with pride, be proud)

- Pride's main plan is to weaken the word of God to the human soul

*Isaiah 24:4...The earth mourneth and fadeth away, the world languisheth and fadeth away, the haughty people of the earth do languish. {the haughty...: Heb. the height of the people}*

- The spirit of Pride tempts people to put a claim to Godly talent and provision.

Deuteronomy 8:16...Who fed thee in the wilderness with manna, which thy fathers knew not, that he might humble thee, and that he might prove thee, to do thee good at thy latter end; 17 And thou say in thine heart, My power and the might of mine hand hath gotten me this wealth. 18 But thou shalt remember the LORD thy God: for it is he that giveth thee power to get wealth, that he may establish his covenant which he sware unto thy fathers, as it is this day.

*Psalm 24:1...The earth is the LORD'S, and the fulness thereof; the world, and they that dwell therein. For he hath founded it upon the seas, and established it upon the floods.*

- This spirit of Pride set a certain pressure on individuals to go ahead rather than to trust the timing of God

*(Ecclesiastics 7:8) Better is the end of a thing than the beginning thereof: and the patient in spirit is better than the proud in spirit.*

- The spirit of Pride intends to create an environment that resists the presence of God. And God resists the presence of pride.

*Genesis 4:7...If thou doest well, shalt thou not be accepted? and if thou doest not well, **sin** lieth at the door. And unto thee shall be his desire, and thou shalt rule over him.*

- Pride leads to the trust of one's own sacrifice rather than obedience to God's provided ways.

*Provers 3:5-6...Trust in the LORD with all thine heart; and lean not unto thine own understanding. In all thy ways acknowledge him, and he shall direct thy paths.*

# Chapter 36

# SPIRIT OF OPPRESSION & TORMENT (ACT 16:23-26)

*(Psalm 72:1) A Psalm for Solomon: Give the king thy judgments, O God, and thy righteousness unto the king's son. 2 ¶ He shall judge thy people with righteousness, and thy poor with judgment. 3 The mountains shall bring peace to the people, and the little hills, by righteousness. 4 He shall judge the poor of the people, he shall save the children of the needy, and shall break in pieces the oppressor.*

True righteous leadership equips, empowers and embraces the people's strengths. Whereas ungodly leaders aim to oppress, control and torment the people into submission. They make every effort to hamper creativity and discourages innovation. Often time, individuals may be talented and very smart as it were, yet, are held under this spirit. It begins by luring it victim by acceptance and goodwill but in the end that web of oppression and torment is cast. They will under achieve and never seem to distinguish themselves in life. It is as though there has been an arrest for development because oppression and torment act like jailors and prisons warden of life.

These can take the shape of procrastination, laziness, addiction, carelessness, un-seriousness and a party spirit of waste.

- The spirit of oppression is a captor… the one that sets people in the prisons of life.
- The spirit of the oppressor is the spirit of the jailer - who would even kill himself when his prisons escape. In other words, it has no plans to let anyone escape but with Jesus all chains are broken
- The spirit of oppression is the fowler that sets a snare

  *Psalm 91:3…Surely he shall deliver thee from the snare*
  *of the **fowler**, and from the noisome pestilence.*

- The spirit of oppression is the oppressor of gifts and talents

  *Matthew 25:25…And I was afraid, and went and hid*
  *thy talent in the earth: lo, there thou hast that is thine*

- The spirit of oppression is the strengthener and the keeper of the prison doors… the spirit that strengthens bondage

  *(Isaiah 14:16) They that see thee shall narrowly look*
  *upon thee, and consider thee, saying, Is this the*
  *man that made the earth to tremble, that did shake*
  *kingdoms; 17 That made the world as a wilderness, and*
  *destroyed the cities thereof; that opened not the house*
  *of his prisoners?*

- The spirit of oppression is the tormentor that uses the spirit of fear

  *(1 John 4:18) There is no fear in love; but perfect love casteth out fear: because fear hath torment. He that feareth is not made perfect in love.*

- The spirit of oppression is the elements under which many operate (Galatians 4:3) Even so we, when we were children, were in bondage under the elements of the world: {elements: or, rudiments}

  … that word "elements" or "stoicheions" refers to something in an orderly or a systematic arrangement. The world will say trouble comes in 3s - that is a confession from the pit of hell; yet the world is unaware of how true that expression is. In order words, satan is not haphazard - there is a method to his madness… there is character to his craziness.

  But he has failed on your behalf. Satan is the first serial killer (John 8:44a) Ye are of your father the devil, and the lusts of your father ye will do. He was a murderer from the beginning. In other words, he is a serial in his operations.

  However, the word "elements" can also refer to a substance which consists of only one type of atom. Making its state or formation is easy to understand. This substance can be said to have an elementary feature or needing improvement or development. The scripture calls it, beggarly elements.

*(Galatians 4:9) But now, after that ye have known God, or rather are known of God, how turn ye again to the weak and **beggarly elements**, whereunto ye desire again to be in bondage?*

So, where satan succeeds in some areas, his tactics still remain beggarly in contrast to the kingdom of God. In other words, he deceives people with simple A, B, C, D schemes. Chose today to walk over him by upgrading to the Kingdom of God.

Character of the spirit of oppression:

- This is the enforcer of bondages (But with prayer, it loses its grip)

  *Galatians 5:1... Stand fast therefore in the liberty wherewith Christ hath made us free, and be not entangled again with the yoke of bondage*

- That spirit of oppression is that invisible whip that seems to flog its victims...

  *(Proverb 26:3) A whip for the horse, a bridle for the ass, and a rod for the fool's back.*

- This spirit assignment is to attack the peace of God...but it fails all the time

  *Colossians 3:15...And **let** the **peace** of God rule in your hearts, to the which also ye are called in one body; and be ye thankful.*

*Roman15:33...Now the God of peace be with you all. Amen.*

*Roman 16:20...And the God of peace shall bruise Satan under your feet shortly. The grace of our Lord Jesus Christ be with you. Amen. {bruise: or, tread}*

- That spirit is sent to inflate the pains in life.

*(Revelation 21:4) And God shall wipe away all tears from their eyes; and there shall be no more death, neither sorrow, nor crying, neither shall there be any more pain: for the former things are passed away.KJV*

- Its plan is to carry out satan's harassments.

*Acts 10:38...How God anointed Jesus of Nazareth with the Holy Ghost and with power: who went about doing good, and healing all that were oppressed of the devil; for God was with him. Oppressed also means Harassment.*

- Its plan is to hold the individual as an infant

*Galatians 4:1...Now I say, That the heir, as long as he is a child, differeth nothing from a servant, though he be lord of all.*

The word child is a translation of the word Nepios, which carries the implication of a baby, a dependent, one who needs to be fed and one who is always vulnerable.

A Christian is a convert… a transformed person - one with new inner drive, totally different from where he/she once was (Ephesians 5:8) For ye <u>were sometimes darkness,</u> but now are ye light in the Lord: walk as children of light: Light cannot try to shine, it shines.

The church, although years old, still carries itself as an infant… not as a baby Christian but as an immature one, who refuses to grow in patience, love and understanding, and in knowledge.

## PRAYER POINT

- ➤ (Ps 146:7) Which executeth judgment for the oppressed: which giveth food to the hungry. The LORD looseth the prisoners.
- ➤ Romans 12: 17-19…Repay no one evil for evil. Have regard for good things in the sight of all men. [18] If it is possible, as much as depends on you, live peaceably with all men. [19]Beloved, do not avenge yourselves, but *rather* give place to wrath; for it is written, "Vengeance *is* Mine, I will repay," says the Lord. KJV

# Chapter 37

# DESTRUCTION OF SPIRIT OF FEAR AND TIMIDITY

*(2Timothy 1:7) For God hath not given us the spirit of fear; but of power, and of love, and of a sound mind.*

God denies that He is not the giver of this spirit of fear, therefore let us (Hebrew 2:14) Forasmuch then as the children are partakers of flesh and blood, he also himself likewise took part of the same; that through death he might destroy him that had the power of death, that is, the devil; 15 And deliver them who through fear of death were all their lifetime subject to bondage.

The scripture is clear that the devil uses fear to bring people into bondage.

- The spirit of fear will cause so many to run from the presence of God
- The spirit of fear will cause us to give a false interpretation to the plans of God

- The spirit of fear is the creator of excuses of all types so as to avoid responsibility
- The spirit of fear will cause the melting of the heart in the face of opposition
- The spirit of fear will stand as an opposer of the voice of God
- The spirit of fear will disguise as the voice of reasoning and logic.
- The spirit of fear will cause one to deny the Love of God (1John 4:18) There is no fear in love; but perfect love casteth out fear: because fear hath torment. He that feareth is not made perfect in love.
- The spirit of fear will cause one to focus only on weakness and impossibilities (Job 11:15) For then shalt thou lift up thy face without spot; yea, thou shalt be stedfast, and shalt not fear:
- The spirit of fear will cause faith to be short-circuited

## FEAR HAS MANY FACES (PHOBIA)

Fear of failure/ fear of people, fear of animal, fear of heights, fear of tight places, fear of depth, fear of pain, fear of leadership, fear of work, fear of men, fear of women, fear of death, fear of sickness, fear of crowd, fear of attention, fear of GOD/ fear of water, and fear of insect.

However, where fear is tolerated, faith is contaminated. Fear can mislead many to think it is just a feeling, but the scripture pronounces it to be a spirit. If it is a spirit, then it has a mind and mission. It is intentional and it is sent to derail it victim from faith in God.

# PRAYER POINT

- ➤ (Deuteronomy 3:22) Ye **shall not fear them:** for the LORD your God he shall fight for you.
- ➤ (2Kings 17:35) With whom the LORD had made a covenant, and charged them, saying, Ye shall not fear other gods, nor bow yourselves to them, nor serve them, nor sacrifice to them:

# HOW DO I COMBAT AND DEFEAT FEAR

- ✓ With the love of God.

  *1 John 4:18...There is no fear in **love**; but **perfect love** casts out fear, because fear involves torment. But he who fears has not been made **perfect** in **love**.*

- ✓ By the confession of God Word

  *Romans10:17...So then faith comes by hearing, and hearing by the word of God.*

- ✓ Confidence in the protective and preventive system that God, which is found in the blood of Jesus

  *(Ps 27:3) Though an host should encamp against me, my heart shall not fear: though war should rise against me, in this will I be confident.*

# Chapter 38

# DESTRUCTION OF SPIRIT OF DIVORCE AND SPIRIT OF ABORTION

It is always good to keep in mind that there is the natural and then there is the spiritual realms respectively. According to Hebrews 11: 3, the natural finds its roots in the spiritual realms. Making the activities taking place in the natural such that are a reflection of what is taking place in the spiritual realms. So, when we take things on face value alone, we become life's casualties.

*(Hebrew 11:3) Through faith we understand that the worlds were framed by the word of God, so that things which are seen were not made of things which do appear...*

*(John 6:63) It is the spirit that quickeneth; the flesh profiteth nothing: the words that I speak unto you, they are spirit, and they are life.*

In other words, there is a spiritual dimension to all you see around you with your physical eyes: the seen world was made from the unseen world...

> *(Malachi 2:16) For the LORD, the God of Israel, saith that he hateth putting away: for one covereth violence with his garment, saith the LORD of hosts: therefore take heed to your spirit, that ye deal not treacherously.*

> *(Matthew 5:31) It hath been said, Whosoever shall put away his wife, let him give her a writing of divorcement:32 But I say unto you, That whosoever shall put away his wife, saving for the cause of fornication, causeth her to commit adultery: and whosoever shall marry her that is divorced committeth adultery.*

> *(Mathew 19:8) He saith unto them, Moses because of the hardness of your hearts suffered you to put away your wives: but from the beginning it was not so.*

> Another word for divorce is "to put away"

> *(Malachi 2:16) For the LORD, the God of Israel, saith that he (b) hateth putting away: for one covereth (c) violence with his garment, saith the LORD of hosts: therefore take heed to your spirit, that ye deal not treacherously.*

## THE NATURE OF THE SPIRIT OF DIVORCE

- The spirit of divorce is violent in nature. It operates in the realms of the spirit of death

- The spirit of divorce is released to tear a person away from enjoying long term investments
- The spirit of divorce violently instigates people to cover their faults and mistakes

*(Psalms 66:18) If I regard iniquity in my heart, the Lord will not hear me:*

- The spirit of divorce instigates the betrayal of trust (its job is to lead the individual to treachery

*(Malachi 2:16... For the* Lord, *the God of Israel, saith that he hateth putting away: for one covereth violence with his garment, saith the* Lord *of hosts: therefore take heed to your spirit, that ye deal not treacherously) therefore take heed to your spirit, that ye deal not treacherously. This means: to violate the faith, to betray of trust.*

- The intention of the spirit of divorce is to instigate one to drop what is precious for a replacement (for instance the wife who has given a man children, discarded by the man after becoming worn out by years of childbearing and domestic duty.)
- The ultimate desire for divorce is to make a person spiritually naked "Covereth violence with his garment... heapeth violence upon his garment," garment here is taken figuratively for wife as in the reference of wife in Genesis 20: 15-16; Ruth 3:9 ; and Ezekiel 16:8 as "GARMENT"
- This spirit of divorce is also a spirit of disgrace... for it tries to expose the believer to ridicule. You shall not be... As a pastor

who is not married… pray and rebuke it for the future…not only those who are married get divorced.

- This spirit operates on singles as well, where before they even go for the first date, that ugly spirit is already stirring up a putting away…I am not saying we should go ahead and grab a partner by force…Listen but there is a place where humility and prayer will help open our eyes and break its grip and allow God to make us hold on until we have a testimony.

*Job 14:14…If a man die, shall he live again? all the days of* **my** *appointed time will I wait,* **till my change** *come.*

- This spirit has instigated certain government laws that give it a place in the home of newlyweds. This law gives the couple the feeling and an easy option to opt out at the slightest stress. How we need Godly leaders to stand against the wickedness of satan.

*2 Chronicles 26:5…And he sought God in the days of Zechariah, who had understanding in the visions of God: and as long as he sought the LORD, God made him to prosper.*

The spirit of divorce will stir the heart to give up. It attacks the individual's strength and first conviction. stirring him/her to give up his/her first love in marriage and in life as a whole.

*(Revelation 2:4) Nevertheless I have somewhat against thee, because thou hast left thy first love. 5 Remember therefore from whence thou art fallen, and repent, and do the first works; or else I will come unto thee quickly, and will remove thy candlestick out of his place, except*

*thou repent. (Proverb 24:10) If thou faint in the day of adversity, thy strength is small.*

- The spirit of divorce disregards help and advice.

*(Proverb 24:6) For by wise counsel thou shalt make thy war: and in multitude of counsellors there is safety.*

*(Proverb 28:13) He that covereth his sins shall not prosper: but whoso confesseth and forsaketh them shall have mercy.*

- The end goal of the spirit of divorce is to destabilize your seeds. It does not only attack the immediate family but its intention is to destabilize the next generation - that they may not find their way back. (Psalm 78:6) That the generation to come might know them, even the children which should be born; who should arise and declare them to their children:
- The spirit of divorce lives and works with one purpose in mind – to stop the next generation from producing that holy seed for God.
  - Most people who come out of a separated family will end up separating.
  - Most people who see their father giving up will end up giving up.
  - Most people who see their parents never try, will themselves never understand how to break-through barriers.
  - Most people are satisfied with giving up and stopping the fight rather than do all they can.
  - Fast, pray, worship. After that fast, pray, worship again; and then again and again and again (Ephesian

6:13) Wherefore take unto you the whole armour of God, that ye may be able to withstand in the evil day, and having done all, **to stand. 14... Stand therefore**, having your loins girt about with truth, and having on the breastplate of righteousness;

- (Philippians 4:4) <u>Rejoice in the Lord always</u>: and again <u>I say, Rejoice.</u>

# Chapter 39

# DESTRUCTION OF SPIRIT OF ABORTION

*(Exodus 23:26) There shall nothing cast their young, nor be barren, in thy land: the number of thy days I will fulfil. (KJV)*

There are two types of abortion:

1.  There is the voluntary abortion where the embryo or fetus is removed from the uterus in order to end a pregnancy.
2.  There is the spontaneous abortion otherwise known as miscarriage

Abortion is the termination of life. Everybody created by God is made for a specific reason and carries God's mission and vision for the planet. Abortion is seen by God, as violence against the weak and vulnerable. It is to take advantage of the voiceless. It is the process of flushing away from Gods plans and purposes away from earth.

Every time satan succeeds to kill; he stops God's attempts to silence prophetic voices, sent to redeem the land from decadence. We will always need fresh voices on the planet and our generation have taken side with the enemy on many fronts.

Just as Pharaoh and Herod went after Moses and Jesus, there is a mass movement of spiritual Pharaohs and Herods in the campaign of ending prophetic voices. But they will not be successful. Whenever there is a Moses, there will be a Pharaoh. Whenever there is Jesus, there will be a Herod. So prayer is of the essence in order to shield our future Moseses and Jesuses

No doubt abortion is a sensitive subject to deal with. Society has myriads of logical reasons why it should be performed; (for instance baby outside wedlock (in some cultures); parents incapable of caring for the baby; baby likely to have an inferior quality of life; fetus unable to survive outside the mother's womb; danger to the mother; child conceived in a rape situation but these are not the norm. At large the promiscuity is to be blamed in many cases and satan is at the root of it all). The Bible is clear about the fact that a child is God's plan - even before its conception. For instance:

- ✓ Firstly: When God refers to humanity, He does not say 'human beings'. He uses such terms as "man / woman / son / daughter / baby / infant". These terms He uses for unborn children.

- ✓ Secondly: the Bible never makes a distinction between fetus and children

✓ Thirdly: the scripture is clear about this point: Body without spirit is dead (James 2:26) Therefore everywhere this is movement and it is life form, it carries God signet.

✓ Fourthly: the blood is the life: (Deuteronomy 12:23)

**Biblical Evidence Of Life In The Womb**

✓ Scripture refers to the unborn in Rebekah's wombs as two nations, struggling inside her. As far as God is concern, He addresses these babies as nations. Anyone who terminates a life has simply terminated a national plan from God (Genesis 25: 21,22)

✓ (Job 3:3) Let the day perish wherein I was born, and the night in which it was said, There is a "man" child conceived. Even though this text is born out of Job's pain; it connotes the emphasis the he was called a man in the womb prior to birth. He went further in stressing, (Job 3:16) Or as a hidden untimely birth I had not been; as infants which never saw light. So He refers here to a life. Saying, yes even if he has not seen light yet, does not remove the facts, that there is an existence already.

✓ John the Baptist, whom God sent ahead of Jesus as a forerunner. He was to prepare his listeners' hearts to receive the messiah. As an infant in the womb, we saw him responding to service as he jumped for joy when both mothers came in contact. Luke 1.

✓ Samson's mother was given strict diets in order to preserve the baby in the womb. Samson was a child of promise. God called him Nazarene from the womb. He did not have to be on the ground to walk in his God given assignment. Judges 13

✓ God called and ordained Jeremiah way before he was found in his mother's womb. This is the most powerful, to even conceive that Jeremiah already had his head anointed in the spirit for an earthly assignment. This is why Abortion is flying-in-your-face rebellion against God. Jeremiah 1:4-5

✓ In the words of Eve, may humanity find the first steps to understanding the purpose of life in the womb in God perspectives;

*Genesis 4:1...And Adam knew Eve his wife; and she conceived, and bare Cain, and said, I have gotten a man from the LORD. Here is another translation... The man Adam knew his wife Eve intimately. She became pregnant and gave birth to Cain, and said, "I have given life to a man with the LORD's help.*

So, it is true, we have babies and they look, speak and behave like us, yet it is by the help of God that we actually get to participate in this beautiful life process.

## THE NATURE OF THE SPIRIT OF ABORTION

As in the physical, so is it in the spirit. There is a deliberate attempt by the enemy to forcefully remove from the womb of your spirit, your spiritual fetus, or pregnancy. Your vision and your dream are compared to fetus. You may not see your vision in the natural but it is alive and doing great in the spirit realms waiting to be birthed.

The spirit of abortion is a violence spirit, targeting to deliver a deadly blow to the dreams and callings of the individual at its embryo stage.

This spirit of abortion carries the same nature as the spirit of death and hell, except that this spirit of abortion has a specific assignment to target the fetus stage.

As we have already compared, in the spirit realm fetuses are dreams, vision, thoughts, ideas, and prophecies by the word of God.

Isaiah 55:11...So shall **my word** be that goeth forth out of my mouth: it shall not return unto me void, but it shall accomplish that which I please, and it shall prosper in the thing whereto I sent it.

In order words, the word of God spoken into the spirit of man becomes that holy conception that The Lord wants to see come into fullness.

(Luke 1:38) And Mary said, Behold the handmaid of the Lord; be it unto me according to thy word. And the angel departed from her

As soon as the word is release, the enemy rages in anger to try and cause abortion of the plan of God. Satan releases his forces. Masked in everyday life difficult, disease and unfortunate conditions of life, he tries to beat people into succumbing to a life of mediocrity and compliance. People become contained and give up trying. I will love to encourage you, to the end that you will not give up and keep on challenging the resistance.

## 4 STATES OF ABORTION

1.  **Abortive condition**... the first 12 weeks is crucial to a child's development. Radiation, viruses, and drugs can cause

abnormalities in the central nervous system and eyes; and viruses can cause deafness and cardiac malformation.

The mother's womb is said to be the safest spot on the planet for the baby. It is in these environments of nurture that the baby needs to continue to grow to attain a mature and healthy baby.

2. **Abortive Nutrition...** some people, unaware of their pregnant condition, have taken drugs – resulting in the loss of their pregnancy. Likewise, in the spirit, one turn or move can mean harm or a blessing.

   We need spiritual nutrition when we come to know Christ. Your vision is strong as the light you carry. It is as powerful as your understanding. Your spiritual diet determines how your vision grows and takes shape.

   I pray for you the blessing.

   *(1Peter 2:2) As newborn babes, desire the sincere milk of the word, that ye may grow thereby.*

   *(Jeremiah 15:16) Thy words were found, and I did eat them; and thy word was unto me the joy and rejoicing of mine heart: for I am called by thy name, O LORD God of hosts. (John 6:54) Whoso eateth my flesh, and drinketh my blood, hath eternal life; and I will raise him up at the last day: 55 For my flesh is meat indeed, and my blood is drink indeed*

3. **Abortive situations** are places and situations that will hurt your walk with God, and will end up aborting that which

you have, for long, conceived. (1King 13:14) And went after the man of God, and found him sitting under an oak: and he said unto him, Art thou the man of God that camest from Judah? And he said, I am.

4. **Abortive agents** (1King 13:8) He said unto him, I am a prophet also as thou art; and an angel spake unto me by the word of the LORD, saying, Bring him back with thee into thine house, that he may eat bread and drink water. But he lied unto him

## SEVEN GOALS OF THE SPIRIT OF ABORTION

1. TO PREVENT GOD GREAT REDEMPTION PLAN (Mathew 1:21) And she shall bring forth a son, and thou shalt call his name JESUS: for he shall save his people from their sins. (WHAT HAS GOD BROUGHT YOUR FORTH TO DO?)

2. TO HINDER OR STOP YOUR VOICE OF PROPHECY (Habakkuk 2:3) For the vision is yet for an appointed time, but at the end it shall speak, and not lie: though it tarry, wait for it; because it will surely come, it will not tarry.

3. TO FRUSTRATE YOUR FUTURE DEVELOPMENT (Isaiah 40:31) But they that wait upon the LORD shall renew their strength; they shall mount up with wings as eagles; they shall run, and not be weary; and they shall walk, and not faint.

4. TO CAUSE UPON YOU A LOAD TOO HEAVY TO BRING INTO THE FURTURE (Matthew 28:11)

5. TO DISARM THE FORCE OF RIGHTEOUSNESS (Isaiah 61:3) To appoint unto them that mourn in Zion, to give unto them beauty for ashes, the oil of joy for mourning, the

garment of praise for the spirit of heaviness; that they might be called trees of righteousness, the planting of the LORD, that he might be glorified.

6.  TO CAUSE REGRET IN THE SOUL: a broken soul cannot carry destiny (Psalm 23:3)

7.  TO BLIND YOU TO THE SEED OF GOD IN YOU… TO CAUSE DISTRACTION

# Chapter 40

# SPIRIT OF SHAME

The spirit of Shame is the laughing voice of mockery.

The spirit of shame is that highlighter of faults and cracks in life.

The spirit of Shame is that veil that covers the individual.

The spirit of shame is a defaming spirit.

The spirit of shame is the picker of quarrels.

The spirit of shame is the sarcastic voice.

The spirit of shame will kill all forms of expressions of thanksgiving.

The spirit of shame is responsible for the creation of small sins.

The spirit of shame is the finger that points to issues that are already under the Blood.

The spirit of shame will be used by the enemy to show nakedness.

The spirit of shame seeks to embarrass the individual with sudden down-turns.

The spirit of shame seeks to make one work without achievement (Ruth 2:15) And when she was risen up to glean, Boaz commanded his young men, saying, Let her glean even among the sheaves, and reproach her not: {reproach...: Heb. shame her not}

# PRAYER POINT

> ➤ (2Ch 32:21) And the LORD sent an angel, which cut off all the mighty men of valour, and the leaders and captains in the camp of the king of Assyria. So he returned with shame of face to his own land. And when he was come into the house of his god, they that came forth of his own bowels slew him there with the sword. {slew...: Heb. made him fall}

The spirit of shame laughs at the losing moment and mocks the winning moment (Psalm 42:10) As with a sword in my bones, mine enemies reproach me; while they say daily unto me, Where is thy God?

The spirit of shame takes on the personality of the accuser of the brethren.

The spirit of shame wants people to laugh at your God. In the environment of shame even the best behavior will slowly adapt to the culture of shame. Understand that shame can be empowering to the wicked at heart because it can be a tool of suppression and intimidation. When God liberate He also destroy the power of shame. You do not have to be ashamed of your past or present condition; know that God the final call.

# BUT YOU WILL LAUGH LAST

*(Psalm 59:11) Slay them not, lest my people forget: scatter them by thy power; and bring them down, O Lord our shield.*

*(Zephaniah 3:19) Behold, at that time I will undo all that afflict thee: and I will save her that halteth, and gather her that was driven out; and I will get them praise and fame in every land where they have been put to shame. {get...: Heb. set them for a praise} {where...: Heb. of their shame}*

The intention of the spirit of shame is to bring a life of weeping and sorrow

*(Psalm 30:5) For his anger endureth but a moment; in his favour is life: weeping may endure for a night, but joy cometh in the morning. {his anger...: Heb. there is but a moment in his anger} {for a night: Heb. in the evening} {joy: Heb. singing}*

The spirit of shame and poverty run together (Proverbs 13:18) Poverty and shame shall be to him that refuseth instruction: but he that regardeth reproof shall be honoured.

## WHEN DOES THE SPIRIT OF SHAME GET AN UPPER HAND?

*(Proverbs 11:2) When pride cometh, then cometh shame: but with the lowly is wisdom.*

When we refuse wise instruction.
When we allow the spirit of pride to rule over us.

When refuse to let go of the past.

When we chose to remain in toxic environments.

When we act on ways that do not align with the will God.

When we see the lens of others.

When we refuse to deal with shameful filters in our minds.

When we unfairly judge ourselves and our achievement.

When we continue to compare our lives with the "highs" of others

When we are not satisfied with the things we have.

When we think poorly of our achievement no matter what they are.

When we refuse to embrace the word of God concerning beauty and love.

# PRAYER POINT

- ➤ **Inherit Glory** (Proverbs 3:35) The wise shall inherit glory: but shame shall be the promotion of fools. (Hosea 4:7) As they were increased, so they sinned against me: therefore will I change their glory into shame.

- ➤ **"I tear all reproach and shame from my face"** (Psalm 69:19) Thou hast known my reproach, and my shame, and my dishonour: mine adversaries are all before thee. (Psalm 119:22) Remove from me reproach and contempt; for I have kept thy testimonies.

# Chapter 41

# Destruction of Spirit of Immorality

*(Genesis 9:20- 21). (1Corinthians 6:13-20) Meats for the belly, and the belly for meats: but God shall destroy both it and them. Now the body is not for fornication, but for the Lord; and the Lord for the body. 14 And God hath both raised up the Lord, and will also raise up us by his own power. 15 Know ye not that your bodies are the members of Christ? shall I then take the members of Christ, and make them the members of a harlot? God forbid. 16 What? know ye not that he which is joined to a harlot is one body? for two, saith he, shall be one flesh. 17 But he that is joined unto the Lord is one spirit. 18 Flee fornication. Every sin that a man doeth is without the body; but he that committeth fornication sinneth against his own body.*

There are three main cravings of the human:

Food

Sleep

Sex

These cravings were initial from God:

- Immorality describes an individual who makes no attempt to curb self-indulgence

  The spirit of immorality stimulates and approves self-indulgence to unlimited degrees

- Immorality describes an individual who has a deprived character, and who voluntarily seeks evil and viciousness

  The spirit of immorality pushes individuals to abandon morals and instead to run after immorality. (1 Corinthians 6:18)

- Immorality also exposes the individual to unrestrained appetite.

  The spirit of immorality aims to break the Godly restraint that leads to a blessed life. (Joel 1:14) Sanctify ye a fast, call a solemn assembly, gather the elders and all the inhabitants of the land into the house of the LORD your God, and cry unto the LORD, {solemn...: or, day of restraint}

  The word **'fast'** is actually a word that describes God's way of teaching the believer to live a life of restraint. So, they who truly fast and pray from the heart can hardly become immoral.

- Immorality is an issue of the heart. (Matthew 15:19-20) (Mathew 5:28) But I say unto you, That whosoever looketh on a woman to lust after her hath committed adultery with her already in his heart.

  The spirit of immorality is to tempt one to sin against one's body – which, at its fullness, leads to death (James 1:15) Then when lust hath conceived, it bringeth forth sin: and sin, when it is finished, bringeth forth death. In other words, when these basic cravings are not restrained by prayer, fasting, and worship, they will lead the believer away from that blessed life. Therefore, unrestraint eating leads to death of the body - diseases. (1 Corinthians 6:13) Unrestrained sleep leads to poverty (lack of vision, lack of finance, laziness) (Proverb 6:10-11) Unrestrained sex (unmarried sex fornication/condemnation) leads to spiritual death (1 Corinthian 6:18).

- The spirit of immorality brings sicknesses and diseases.

- The spirit of immorality will lead to self -worship …

  (Philippians 3:19) Whose end is destruction, whose God is their belly, and whose glory is in their shame, who mind earthly things.

  The spirit of immorality is one of the works of the flesh (Galatians 5:19-21).

- Immorality will ultimately lead to a life of rags (Proverbs 23:21) For the drunkard and the glutton shall come to poverty: and drowsiness shall clothe a man with rags.

# Chapter 42

# SPIRIT OF DRUNKENNESS

runkenness means that an individual is beside themselves - not in control… out of bounds. It is also a state of being intoxicated. A person in such state is usually under the influence of an intoxicating substance. In the spiritual realm, an individual can get intoxicated in that, they can lose themselves to certain excess and in the end loss their religion and spirituality. I pray this will not become of you.

## TYPES OF DRUNKENESS

1. Power drunk
2. Sex drunk
3. Beauty Drunk
4. Money Drunk
5. Position drunk
6. Qualification Drunk
7. Status Drunk
8. Self – drunk
9. Control drunk
10. Attention Drunk

11. Envy drunk
12. Food drunk
13. Alchohol drunk
14. Smoking drunk
15. Outing drunk
16. Shopping Drunk
17. Working Drunk
18. Fame drunk

- The spirit of drunkenness intends to bring to an individual a strange personality.
- The spirit of drunkenness aims to expose an individual to strange attention
- The spirit of drunkenness instigates ungodly words (i.e. it will change your words to curses)

Spirit of drunkenness (intoxication, spiritual intoxication / natural intoxication). This is the state where one is controlled by substance.

Being drunk in the spirit is recommended in the bible. (Ephesians 5:18) And be not drunk with wine, wherein is excess; but be filled with the Spirit.

However, from the life of Noah, we know that drunkenness once more resulted to the release of the curse on the earth. The tendency to become drunk is very high when one does not become temperate to choose to be sober by relaxing in comfort derived from the wisdom provided in God and his word to worldly means of comfort and socializing.

Prayer points in the days when you are tempted to add substance to the find comfort elsewhere.

Colossians 2:10...And ye are complete in him, which is the head of all principality and power:

# Chapter 43

# Destruction of Spirit of Witchcraft and Spirit of Idolatry

*The spirit of witchcraft is otherwise known as the spirit of Mind-Control. (Ezekiel 13:18-21).*

Satan's intention is to collect the minds of all inhabitants of the earth so that in the end he will get them to worship him.

The spirit of witchcraft refers to the casting of spells or conjuring up of spirits on people, whereas God calls for a voluntary relationship.

God warns in the Old Testament in Deuteronomy 18:9-12

9 When you come into the land which the Lord your God gives you, you shall not learn to follow the abominable practices of these nations.10 There shall not be found among you anyone who makes his son or daughter pass through the fire, or who uses divination, or is a

soothsayer, or an augur, or a sorcerer,[11] Or a charmer, or a medium, or a wizard, or a necromancer.[12] For all who do these things are an abomination to the Lord, and it is because of these abominable practices that the Lord your God is driving them out before you.

This spirit of witchcraft causes or leads people to uncontrollable urges and thoughts. (Certain emotions and feelings rise up unexpectedly. The person's personality is marked by serious mood swings.)

The witchcraft spirit literally haunts with memories of the past

The spirit of witchcraft has an entourage of addictions that accompany it, i.e., drugs, alcohol and masturbation

The person upon whom the spell of witchcraft is working will feel compelled to act in certain ways - even without reason! Often, anger and bitterness arise suddenly, and then subsides as though nothing happened.

The spirit of witchcraft is the controllers of physical things through spiritual dimensions - to bring great deception

Deception is one of the greatest weapons of the spirit of witchcraft (1thessalonian 2:3)

In the last days, many will be deceived. Jesus warns of that in Matthew 24:12, 24. And in Revelation 13:14. People who are deceived are people whom witchcraft have fed with so much lies, that lies become their truth (John 8:44)

The witchcraft spirit is responsible for planting lies that will lead to negative and false decisions.

The witchcraft spirit uses hypnosis. Like drugs, chants, devices like games and board games, these are invented by satan as doors and gates to the mind for a total control. Hypnosis is a great avenue for satan to suggest lies. An entire nation can be hypnotized - take Nazi Germany for instance.

The spirit of witchcraft's ultimate goal is to seat that governmental seat to control and govern large territory and to take place that does not belong to it. By nature, it opposes God and wants to function as kings.

1 king 21:7-8...And Jezebel his wife said unto him, Dost thou now govern the kingdom of Israel? arise, *and* eat bread, and let thine heart be merry: I will give thee the vineyard of Naboth the Jezreelite. So she wrote letters in Ahab's name, and sealed *them* with his seal, and sent the letters unto the elders and to the nobles that *were* in his city, dwelling with Naboth.

Evidence of the witchcraft spirit or of mind Control is often headaches or confusion. When this spirit is in operation is causes its victim to feel being unteachableness.

Hardness of mind
Stubbornness
Deep depression yet the excitement of being in control.
Unbelief and suspicion
The spirit of unwillingness to see reason.

# Chapter 44

# DESTRUCTION OF SPIRIT OF DOUBT

*(Luke 1:37) For with God nothing shall be impossible.*

*(Hebrew 3:12) Take heed, brethren, lest there be in any of you an evil heart of unbelief, in departing from the living God*

- Spirit of unbelief or doubt or double mindedness is a power that departs from the Living God. (Hebrew 3:19) So we see that they could not enter in because of unbelief.
- The spirit of Unbelief closes the door to blessings. (Hebrew 4:11) Let us labour therefore to enter into that rest, lest any man fall after the same example of unbelief.
- The spirit of unbelief takes away the rest reserved for those God has called. (Ephesians 5:6) Let no man deceive you with vain words: for because of these things cometh the wrath of God upon the children of disobedience. (Unbelief)
- The spirit of unbelief sponsors disobedience.
- The spirit of unbelief is the root of all sin.

- Unbelief of God's promises will lead to impatience
- Unbelief in God's love will lead to foster love
- Unbelief in God's provisions will lead to lying and stealing
- Unbelief in God's timing will lead to the work and hand of man

*Rom 4:20 He staggered not at the promise of God through unbelief; but was strong in faith, giving glory to God;*

- The spirit of unbelief causes one to walk in inconsistency. That spirit is responsible for failure in the faith. (Mark 6:6) And he marveled because of their unbelief. And he went round about the villages, teaching. Even Jesus wondered at unbelief

- Ultimately, the spirit of unbelief is sent by the enemy to bring embarrassment to the work of God

## PRAYER POINT

- ➢ (Mark 9:24) And straightway the father of the child cried out, and said with tears, Lord, I believe; help thou mine unbelief.

# Chapter 45

# Destroying the Spirit of Low Self-Esteem and Spirit of Failure

Combating the spirit of low self-esteem which leads to all kinds of failure is of the essence in our days. Never in the history of mankind have there been an epidemic of depression like now. Mostly stem from people feeling inadequate, insufficient and in search of something of a life they cannot substantiate.

These are some issues people suffer as a result of having or nurturing low self-esteem.

They will consistently consider themselves lost and unworthy of being cared for.

They struggle in the area of creativity

They are poor faith takers (risk).

They operate out of fear of rejection.

They are hungry for approval of others.

They are poor problem solver — poor solution mentality.

They are flooded with irrational thoughts and operate in irrational thinking.

They are susceptible to all kinds of fear.

They have a tendency to become emotionally stuck and immobilized.

They have a poor track record in school or work… on the flip side they sometime become may over-compensating and become achievers yet will remain unfulfilled.

They are unable to affirm themselves positively being also unable to receive affirmations

They are unable to make an honest assessment of ability or strengths, qualities or good points…

They find it difficult to accept compliments or recognition from others

They become chameleon very easily to fit in with other because of a poor self- identity

They are insecure, anxious, and nervous when they are with others

They often become overcome with anger about their status in life and are likely to have chronic hostility or chronic depression

They can become easily overcome with despair and depression when they experience a set-back or loss in life.

They develop a sense or desire for revenge with those who they feel did not accept them fully.

They are easily de-energize by resentment

They are very vulnerable to mental health problems and have a propensity to use addictive behaviour to medicate their hurt and pain. Suh addictive behaviour can be drugs, alcohol, food, gambling, working too much; a search for excitement, happiness, wrong meditation and so forth.

# YOUR PRAYER POINTS

➢ For the grace of God to flourish in your life and affairs. I pray all that concerns you will be brought to a wonderful end in Jesus Name.

➢ 1Corinthians 15:10...But by the grace of God I am what I am: and his grace which was bestowed upon me was not in vain; but I laboured more abundantly than they all: yet not I, but the grace of God which was with me.

➢ 2Corinthians 3:5... Not that we are sufficient of ourselves to think anything as of ourselves; but our sufficiency is of God;

➢ Colossians 2:8-10 ...'Beware lest any man spoil you through philosophy and vain deceit, after the tradition of men, after the rudiments of the world, and not after Christ. For in him dwelleth all the fulness of the Godhead bodily. And ye are COMPLETE in him, which is the head of all principality and power.'

# Chapter 46

# THE SPIRIT OF DECEPTION

*2 Corinthians 11: 3...But I fear, lest by any means, as the serpent beguiled Eve through his subtilty, so your minds should be corrupted from the simplicity that is in Christ.*

eguile is a bit of an old English word for trickery, or to deceive or deception. In the Cambridge dictionary, deception defined as the act of hiding the truth, especially to get an advantage.

Satan's chief strategy is deception. It is about time to stand against all his deception in the church and start to fight the fight against the enemy and not ourselves. The Love of God includes the believer in all promises. There is now no more condemnation to those who are in Christ. However, the enemy will take advantage of certain unfortunate events and try to manipulate us into thinking negative concerning God's Love. The word subtility points to his relentless effort to turn man against the truth of God's word at all levels.

However, it is the truth that can set one free from his grand deceptive plans. Jesus withstood satan with the truth of God's word in the wilderness, as He (Jesus) recounted God's words, "it is written".

John 8:32...And ye shall know the truth, and the truth shall make you free.

# THE DIFFERENT MANIFESTATIONS OF THE SPIRIT OF DECEPTION

1. Word deception.

> *(Ephesians 5:6) Let no man deceive you with vain words: for because of these things cometh the wrath of God upon the children of disobedience.*

Satan will use people to speak deceptive words to you and make you feel wrong about the right things. He is known for such trickery. There was hi trick in the garden of Eden, he spoke contrary words and deceived Eve. Often times, we make the worst of little issue. Only to find out how over reactive we have been. Many marriages will still be intact till date only if word would have been controlled and wrong counsel avoided.

Pray:   Lord expose all evil counsel.

Lord I put a watch over my mouth not to allow evil and deceptive find expression.

Lord Shine a light all evil word and evil suggestion.

Lord all evil word in operation in my life now; I put a stop it by the blood of Jesus.

2. Human Disception...

*(Ephesians 4:14) That we henceforth be no more children, tossed to and fro, and carried about with every wind of doctrine, by the sleight of men, and cunning craftiness, whereby they lie in wait to deceive;*

Sad to say there are many lying in wait, to take advantage of you. They may be friends, colleagues, salesmen even loved ones, who may have good intentions but the human nature warrants uncertainties. The scripture says "God is not man that HE should lie", pointing to the fact that wherever mans is there is a tendency for lies, exaggeration or pretenses. We all do not know the future, hence many become desperate and prone to using deception. In business today, integrity is no longer the norm. Many want to make it fast and easy.

3. Self Disception...

*(1John 1:8) If we say that we have no sin, we deceive ourselves, and the truth is not in us.*

This is having a false sense of reality. This is a lack of objectivism, where an individual will refuse to face fact in the name of faith. Faith does not cancel fact but faith overrules facts. Yet, there must be fact somewhere to be over-ruled, excuse my repetition. Avoid becoming an imposter, an actor and one who plays a role. You have a unique life and destiny. Find your real-ness and rip off the mask today.

Satan tempts people to compete with their neighbors, friends or family to the extent of losing their personality in the process. There are times and seasons for everything under the sun, somethings can just not happen until the Lord moves on it. "Fake it till you make it" is a popular term out there, I will suggest that you, faith it until you make it.

In the book of Hebrews, it says by Faith…

Be yourself. If you do not know who you are, study Christ, you are being formed into the image of Christ.

4. Gifting Deception

This is so prevalent in the body of Christ in these last days. What is called the projection of gifting? The scripture is clear about esteeming others more than ourselves. It also gives, to be sober and level headed. We can become deceived in thinking that we have the best gift on the block and start walking in the spirit of entitlement. Many have assumed the seat of the teacher and correctors in the body, when they should really be students. There is a place for honour and our generation need to find this place again. The date toll in the body among your preacher is really frightening; we should still study and consider, Ephesians 6:1-2...Honour thy father and mother; which is the first commandment with promise; That it may be well with thee, and thou mayest live long on the earth. Length of days may not only constitute longevity but also the favour on the work of the ministry.

Phil 2: 3 / 1Peter 5:8-9

5. World Disception.

> *(Revelation 20:7) And when the thousand years are expired, Satan shall be loosed out of his prison, 8 And shall go out to deceive the nations which are in the four*

*quarters of the earth, Gog and Magog, to gather them together to battle: the number of whom is as the sand of the sea.*

How are people being deceived by the phenomena in the world today? Everything so fast you would really wish you ask the whole thing to stop and wait for you. In the midst of the rush, important decision needs to be made. The deadlines to assignments, family and work project, investments, your spiritual life and so on. In all these happenings, beware not go with the flow and be deceived with the crowd.

6. Wealth /Material Disception..

*(Mark 4:19) And the cares of this world, and the deceitfulness of riches, and the lusts of other things entering in, choke the word, and it becometh unfruitful. 1Timothy 6:17...Charge them that are rich in this world, that they be not high-minded, nor trust in uncertain riches, but in the living God, who giveth us richly all things to enjoy;*

Riches must have its rightful place in your life. Where we know that wealth and riches are good, they are not God. It has its place in life's affairs but it cannot be substituted for the grace of God.

# Chapter 47

# Spirit of Division

*Ephesians 2:14...Christ has made peace between Jews and Gentiles, and he has united us by breaking down the wall of hatred that separated us. Christ gave his own body*

Division is the action of separating something into parts or the process of being separated as defined by online dictionary. The second definition is also worth considering difference or disagreement between two or more groups, typically producing tension.

One of the reasons people lack the courage to wait in prayer is the feeling of being separated from God even after being born again. Satan still holds the past of many and creates a wall of separation between believers and their blessings. This spirit preys on our past life of darkness and ignorant actions. This is the language of what should have, and what could have been. This spirit enters into persistent dialogue with emphasis on the pain of the consequence from our actions.

It is a mindset of victims. The victim's mind creates walls to solution and talks down at the language of responsibility. The walls in general were created by the sin of Adam, leading humanity down the path of division.

The division of God and man

The division of God and his planet

The division of Man and Woman (until there is a decision to get married)

The division of man and his environment

The division of animal life forms

The division between the human system of life

The division between the spirit, soul and spirit

The division of life from the earth

This division is a spirit felt at all levels of life. Notice, we must interact and gain mastery at all these levels in other get ahead in life. Sometime, we may feel disarmed and unqualified to access the blessings of the Lord. Be aware of this spirit.

When it comes to the socio-geographically environment, humanity have suffered the brunt of deep-seated division between cultures, tribes and people group. People groups have been thrown into wars and conflict for generations and sad to say it still does.

This condition takes its root from this spirit that divides. Do not allow your destiny to be hindered because of your background or your frontier, break the containments today and move ahead and become all God has designed you to be.

> *Ephesians 2:12-13...That at that time ye were without Christ, being aliens from the commonwealth of Israel, and strangers from the covenants of promise, having no hope, and without God in the world:[13] But now in Christ Jesus ye who sometimes were far off are made nigh by the blood of Christ.*

In all these prayers, you are courting your heart with the love of God. You are no longer an enemy of God. You have been reconciled and His worth has been placed on your life. You can be raised to new heights. You can do new and worthy things. You can move from being and feeling unworthy to a person of value and worth because Christ has removed all walls of hatred.

# Chapter 48

# DESTRUCTION OF SPIRIT OF RAPE

- The spirit of rape and harassment is a brutal spirit sent from hell and imposed on individual in order to cause a deep sense of loss.
- The spirit of rape and harassment seeks to impose on people by forcefully removing the dignity in life.
- The spirit of rape and harassment is the personality of the Devil (John 10:10)
- The spirit which Jesus deals with in (Act 10:3) How God anointed Jesus of Nazareth with the Holy Ghost and with power: who went about doing good, and healing all that were **oppressed** of the devil; for God was with him.

OPPRESSED: (katadunasteuo. To exercise dominion over, to harass). When there is RAPE AND HARASSMENT, the oppressor will always take the possession of the victim by force. To instigate abandonment and misfortune.

- The spirit of rape and harassment will use events, occasions, opportunities, places, and dates and times to frustrate efforts of progress.

- The spirit of rape and harassment's purpose is to steal and diminish one value of self, their gifting, talent and dreams. It is a dream thieve and a dream killer.

- The spirit of rape and harassment can be so audacious as even to set time, date and place of attack — the threat of not even attempting to go forward.

- The spirit of rape and harassment is a time waster and endeavors to bring a fear of all sorts.

- The spirit of rape and harassment devalues, disregards, disrespects and undermines individual propensity of creativity.

- When the spirit of rape and harassment attacks, it always follows a robing away or a tearing away of precious emotional values and blessings. It must be stopped long before it appears.

People can be used intensely by this spirit to maltreat gifted individuals for the gain of personal promotion and visibility: They will go ahead and used gifted people without appreciation and leave them for death. When you talk with people that are spiritually raped, they somehow cannot pull their minds away from past glory. They hold on to the glory of the past because it brings them certain gratification and satisfaction. They will refuse to see the future and the better opportunities that are in front.

This spirit leaves an uncomfortable smell of defeat and shame as well as bitterness against potential collaborators. They are just contained on all side but the power in the blood can change all that. Rehab was in the same situation; she was abuse and stuck within a wall. The wall that protected the city was her small prison, where other felt safe from the elements, she was exposed and naked, it was the place, where she was abused and maltreated but her day of deliverance came and the scarlet thread was her way out. I really pray that you can trust the blood of Jesus Today and you will be set free. See the following chapter for more insight on Rehab's victory.

Joshua 2:17... Now the men had said to her, "This oath you made us swear will not be binding on us [18] unless, when we enter the land, you have tied this scarlet cord in the window through which you let us down, and unless you have brought your father and mother, your brothers and all your family into your house. [19] If any of them go outside your house into the street, their blood will be on their own heads; we will not be responsible. As for those who are in the house with you, their blood will be on our head if a hand is laid on them. [20] But if you tell what we are doing, we will be released from the oath you made us swear." [21] "Agreed," she replied. "Let it be as you say." So she sent them away, and they departed. And she tied the scarlet cord in the window. NIV

# Chapter 49

# DESTRUCTION OF SPIRIT OF HARLOTRY AND PROSTITUTION

There is a great story of a harlot in the Bible named Rahab. She was a residence of Jericho at the time when Israel were on the exodus to the Promised Land. God has promised to give Israel favour and spiritual might to conquer any nation which stood against this process. Jericho happens to be one of those nations.

Two spies where sent to spy out Jericho because it will not offer a passageway. The Bible says it was tightly shut because of the Israelite. Theses spies where exposed and in danger, but Rahab sheltered them and even lied to save their lives. So, God can use your hospitality for good therefore you need prayer to safe guard yourself from this abusive spirit.

Insight on the operation of the spirits:

This is the spirit of broken hospitality

This spirit undermines the gift of reception and abuses goodwill.

This spirit defames the power to lead.

This spirit cripples the power to bring real comfort in service.

This spirit is a spirit of abuse and dishonour

This spirit aims to all steal beauty (Spiritually, emotionally and physically).

This spirit aims to lead into an undignified life

This is spirit which amplifies the physical rather the inner quality of people

This is the governor of superficiality

This spirit promotes the spirit of rebellion (in the case of Samson and Delilah)

This spirit breaks down moral boundaries.

In the end Rehabs was rewarded through her gift of hospitality. The enemy tried to rape and destroy her life by the hand of wicked and immoral men, but in the end she re-gain her place in life by the same gift and service to bring the messiah into the world. So, it is a victory at the end of her life, she was delivered from all these spirits that tried to terminate her destiny. So do not give up or give in, serve your gift to the world and the blood of Jesus will testify for you.

# Chapter 50

# DESTRUCTION OF THE SPIRIT OF DARKNESS

*Romans 13:11-31...You know what sort of times we live in, and so you should live properly. It is time to wake up. You know that the day when we will be saved is nearer now than when we first put our faith in the Lord. $^{12}$ Night is almost over, and day will soon appear. We must stop behaving as people do in the dark and be ready to live in the light. $^{13}$ So behave properly, as people do in the day. Don't go to wild parties or get drunk or be vulgar or indecent. Don't quarrel or be jealous. CEV*

These evil spirits cause slumber in the people's spirit. Slumber a sleeping spirit, just as one sleeping is not cognitive to interactions, the same one slumbering in the spirit cannot receive the word of God. It is a casual carefree spirit toward sacred things and will not revere or respect it. This spirit holds individuals in certain ignorant level for too long. They remain ignorant to themselves and other. The spirit attacks the mind not to be cognizant concerning their circumstances.

This spirit takes advantage of people in depression, denial, stubbornness, open rebellion toward God and His word. It becomes prevalent, because, where the word of God is resisted, darkness prevails. Seeing God is light and the light shines in darkness, when truth is honored and respected, the spirit of darkness will lose its grip.

Darkness is a powerful container that stops so many in the valley of life. It instigates behavioral pattern contrary to developments and maturity, especially in the areas of God's eternal word. Every behavior pattern is instigated by levels of information and revelation. Changing Patterns in behaviour signifies that one has received new revelation. So light will always cause a behaviour shift from darkness

Left in the dark" is a phrase meaning, to be kept uninformed of something or to be excluded from full knowledge or disclosure. The bible says "where there is no vision the people perish." This spirit of darkness robs people of vision and direction. Leadership potential is a target for this spirit. Satan will attempt to hinder and contained great potential by leaving people in darkness of all sorts, but the word says "Jesus is the Light that lighted anyone who comes into the world". So, faith in Jesus is the beginning of challenging darkness. The reference scripture instructs the believers to put the amour of light. Amour is a weapon. It points to light being a weapon of war to combat darkness. This only reveals that darkness is a weapon used to disarm and at times crippling individuals but thank God, there is no comparison with the weapon of light.

# PRAYER:

> ➤ I put the armor of light today.
> ➤ Darkness you have no right of my spirit, soul and body

These are spirits hidden under the dark waters of this world.

The spirit of darkness is a lying spirit.

The spirit of darkness propagates the falsehood of life in general.

The spirit of darkness is an elusive entity that promotes the arrests of development at all levels.

The spirit of darkness is the hidden force of the enemy behind addictive thoughts and tendency

The spirit of darkness is what the bible calls the unfruitful worker, it seizes and hijacks growth of any kind.

Where there is little emotional growth, it is a sign that this spirit is in operation.

The spirit of darkness is a night crawler deceiving individual to commit crime and promising false hope

*(Jeremiah 4:28) For this shall the earth mourn, and the heavens above be black: because I have spoken it, I have purposed it, and will not repent, neither will I turn back from it.*

Only the armour of light can defeat such prevailing darkness. The Bible pray to put on the amour of light of the weapons of light because the day is soon breaking. Meaning never lose sight on your God giving vision which began from the word of God and always continue in the path of light. Vision is key and developing in all areas of your calling in righteousness.

> *Romans 13:12..The night is far spent, the day is at hand: let us therefore cast off the works of darkness, and let us put on the armour of light.*

# Chapter 51

# DESTRUCTION OF SPIRIT OF INTIMIDATION AND TERROR

*Isaiah 54:14…In righteousness shalt thou be established: thou shalt be far from oppression; for thou shalt not fear: and from terror; for it shall not come near thee.*

In our days, there atmosphere is charged with terror or terrorism. The spirit creates a failing heart. The spirit makes one to be a coward, to run away from, to give up or to give in. It is a spirit causing many hearts to fail and refusing to try again.

This is a spirit preventing many from trying again. A failed business, relationship, project and any event where there is a shape cut in heart and mind and the door gets open for this spirit. Where individuals learn not to try again and become discouraged, it is an inner voice speaking against further progress. This is the most strategic of containers, seeing that it is subtle and has a sort-of-positive tone to one's decision.

It can stand before an entire family and nation and operate as a generational curse. Joshua had to be reminded on three occasions by God to be strong and courageous. His is to fight against this spirit head on to break the containment into the promises of God.

> *Joshua 1:6...Be strong and of good courage, for to this people you shall divide as an inheritance the land which I swore to their fathers to give them.*

> *Joshua 1:7...Only be strong and very courageous, that you may observe to do according to all the law which Moses My servant commanded you; do not turn from it to the right hand or to the left, that you may prosper wherever you go.*

> *Joshua 1:9...Have not I commanded thee? Be strong and of a good courage; be not afraid, neither be thou dismayed: for the LORD thy God is with thee whithersoever thou goest.*

After forty years in the wilderness and many battles, then the loss of his mentor, Moses and the feeling most successor will deal with. Moses was not just any predecessor, his work was gigantic, and Joshua had a major shoe to fill. It is obvious that intimidation showed up to contain Joshua.

He was untried as a leader and needed assurance of success. He mediated on God's promises but for some reason was lacking motivation. Intimidation pushes back creativity and innovation. It paralyzes the thought process and makes one frozen and discouraged.

However, God in His great love and wealth of understanding knows where we all are and His words are our only rock in times of intimidation of life. His promise is sure and he will step in the battle at the right time. Jesus preenacted because when Joshua met Him, he addressed himself as **the captain** of the **Lord's host** and then we find that it is the **Lord**! Joshua worshiped Him, and He did not stop Joshua in his worship, rather He commands Joshua to take off His shoes because it is holy ground. The same word his mentor Moses must have relayed to him.

God showed up at the first battle, as a mere man and his sword drawn to take over command of his army. "I am not on any ones side rather you are on my side; Powerful presence. God is on your side and the enemies know this, so do not allow them to intimidate you. Sometime we want to see supernatural acts, however, it is in prayer that we discover God's wisdom. In prayer, we learn to participate in divine assignments and accomplishments.

> *Joshua 5:13...And it came to pass, when Joshua was by Jericho, that he lifted up his eyes and looked, and, behold, there stood a man over against him with his sword drawn in his hand: and Joshua went unto him, and said unto him, Art thou for us, or for our adversaries? 14 And he said, Nay; but as captain of the host of the LORD am I now come. And Joshua fell on his face to the earth, and did worship, and said unto him, What saith my Lord unto his servant? 15 And the captain of the LORD's host said unto Joshua, Loose thy shoe from off thy foot; for the place whereon thou standest is holy. And Joshua did so.*

# Epilogue

God designed us for success by wiring into each one with great minds, personalities and talents. Prayer activates these powers. Life is the container we find ourselves in. Which try to contain your dreams and callings by myriads of events and effects; which tend to keep us distracted from finding our main calling in life.

Life should not determine what we do or become; we are to determine how life treats us and what we become in life. In prayer, we begin to set the tone of our life. We learn to resist temptations to settle and remain contained. God knows our potential to raise to great heights and he is not shy about it. Hence his invitation to pray for answers and breakthrough.

It is left for you to challenge yourselves by strategic prayers. You are delivered into the world not to talk and keep your dreams inside of you but be revealed as it were and to present the gift of God in you. As it is said, "do not judge the book by its cover". Your cover only will not serve the purpose of God. So, the world is waiting to enjoy your content as well.

"…One Of His Disciple
Said Unto Him

"Lord Teach Us To Pray"